#1 ART VERONICA

FAME

DAVID GRITTEN

FAME
Stripping Celebrity Bare

ALLEN LANE
an imprint of
PENGUIN BOOKS

ALLEN LANE
THE PENGUIN PRESS

Published by the Penguin Group
Penguin Books Ltd, 80 Strand, London WC2R ORL, England
Penguin Putnam Inc., 375 Hudson Street, New York, New York 10014, USA
Penguin Books Australia Ltd, 250 Camberwell Road, Camberwell, Victoria 3124, Australia
Penguin Books Canada Ltd, 10 Alcorn Avenue, Toronto, Ontario, Canada M4V 3B2
Penguin Books India (P) Ltd, 11, Community Centre, Panchsheel Park, New Delhi – 110 017, India
Penguin Books (NZ) Ltd, Cnr Rosedale and Airborne Roads, Albany, Auckland, New Zealand
Penguin Books (South Africa) (Pty) Ltd, 24 Sturdee Avenue, Rosebank 2196, South Africa

Penguin Books Ltd, Registered Offices: 80 Strand, London WC2R ORL, England

www.penguin.com

First published 2002

1

Copyright © David Gritten, 2002

The moral right of the author has been asserted

All rights reserved. Without limiting the rights under copyright
reserved above, no part of this publication may be reproduced, stored in
or introduced into a retrieval system, or transmitted, in any form or by
any means (electronic, mechanical, photocopying, recording or otherwise),
without the prior written permission of both the copyright owner
and the above publisher of this book

Set in 10.5/14 pt Linotype Sabon
Typeset by Rowland Phototypesetting Ltd, Bury St Edmunds, Suffolk
Printed in England by Clays Ltd, St Ives plc

ISBN 0-713-99536-X

For Sally

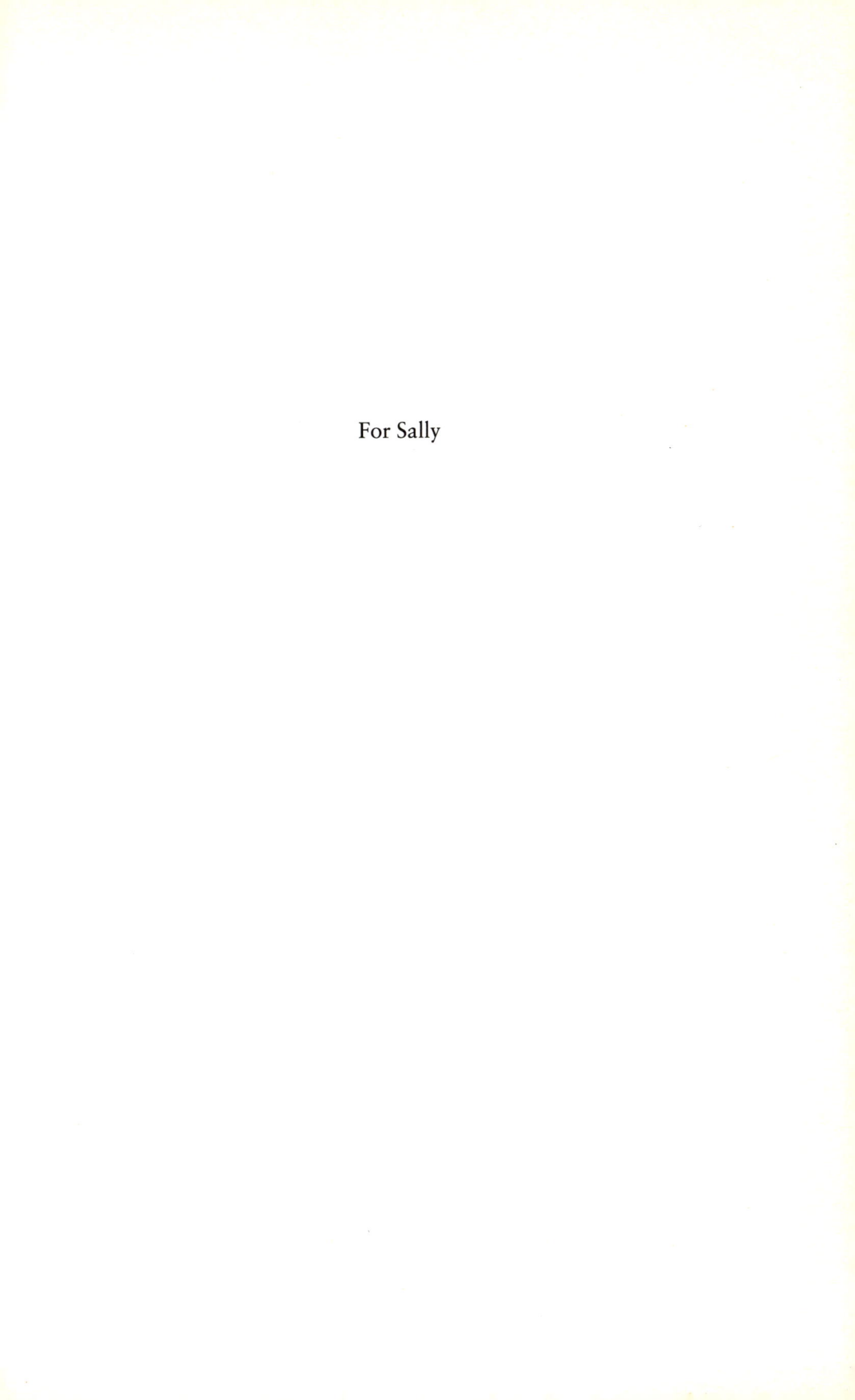

Contents

1. The Fame Dilemma — 1
2. Fame Becomes a Problem — 14
3. Who Needs Fame? — 28
4. The Fans — 42
5. The Media — 57
6. Everybody's Famous — 71
7. Playing at Fame — 85
8. Involuntary Fame — 99
9. Flourishing with Fame — 113
10. The Pitfalls of Fame — 126
11. Privacy — 140
12. Conclusion — 153

I

The Fame Dilemma

RULE ONE:
Fame's consequences are always complex

In 1999 the actress Julia Roberts was approached by Tigress Productions, a British production company that makes hour-long wildlife documentaries for television. The company had a request: would she like to spend three weeks on the bleak, arid plains of Mongolia, observing that country's wild horses? Tigress sends camera crews to remote parts of the world to film indigenous animals or birds, but adds an audience-friendly twist; a film star goes along to act as presenter and comment on the wildlife through the eyes of a lay person. Actors Anthony Hopkins, Robin Williams, Goldie Hawn and Whoopi Goldberg were among those who had taken part.

Andrew Jackson, who runs Tigress, had good reason for contacting Roberts. She was, after all, the world's most famous and highly-paid film actress, having starred in a string of hits – *Pretty Woman, My Best Friend's Wedding, Notting Hill* and *Runaway Bride* among them. Her mere presence on screen would be enough to increase the appeal of the documentary among TV audiences worldwide. But there was another factor. Filming for three weeks on the remote Mongolian steppes would be especially gruelling, and Jackson knew Roberts was up to the task. She had already presented a Tigress documentary about tigers in Borneo, and proved herself adaptable; she travelled light, exhibited few of the petulant whims with which one often associates movie stars, and was both friendly and co-operative with the camera crew. She had also been a sensitive, thoughtful tourist who respected the culture and environment of the countries to which she travelled.

All these attributes would prove necessary. Roberts and the five-person crew were to live with a family of nomadic horse herders on the steppe, and she had to share all their chores – looking after their children, chopping mutton, milking the mares. It is a life of extraordinary hardship. The family live in huge, brightly painted circular tents, which they expertly dismantle in a matter of minutes and move on in search of new pasture for their horses. They huddle around meagre wood fires in bitterly cold winters made harsher by northerly winds from Siberia. There are no toilet facilities; they simply walk outside and squat on the plains.

Still, Roberts responded to the challenge, arriving at the airport of Mongolia's capital, Ulan Bator, carrying only one light rucksack and dressed plainly in jeans and an Arctic jacket. She did not look so different from the hundreds of young backpackers who visit Mongolia each year. Roberts and the crew met up and endured a bumpy sixty-mile ride across the steppes in an old truck with hard seats to find the host family. There were no roads, fences or maps, and no guarantee of where this family might be; they could have moved from their last known encampment to a new pasture. Finally they found each other, and were introduced through translators. The female members of the family decided Roberts's Western clothes would be insufficient for the weather's rigours, and lent her a crimson *del*, a long jacket of padded silk designed to exclude the bitingly cold wind.

Shooting started that same day; Roberts was filmed tentatively sipping at fermented mare's milk, which tastes like fizzy yoghurt. But something was clearly wrong, the family's attitude seemed tentative and suspicious. On the second day its patriarch, a veteran horse herder named Henmedeh, approached the English director Nigel Cole looking confused and upset, to say he was sure a trick was being played on him and his family.

'Why?' asked an astonished Cole.

The old man explained that on one of his rare visits to Ulan Bator, he had seen Julia Roberts in *Pretty Woman* on video. And he did not believe that this young woman could be that same Julia Roberts.

'Henmedeh had an idea of what a film star was,' said Cole. 'He imagined a ball gown, a limo, a red carpet, a haughty air. He expected to be intimidated and overawed by Julia. Because she turned out to be so relaxed, casually dressed and not at all regal, he couldn't believe she was so internationally famous.' Roberts, in other words, had temporarily shed her celebrity persona, a role-playing exercise in which famous people indulge to varying extents when they present themselves, or a selective version of themselves, to the public; in Mongolia, she was simply an ordinary citizen.

Henmedeh's mistake concerning Roberts indicates that hers is an example of fame at its most extreme. It is one thing to show up at a premiere of your new film, where crowds line the street and watch your arrival to the pop of a hundred photographers' flash bulbs. It is one thing to be unable to walk down a street of any city in your own country without being harassed and jostled by fans. And it is one thing to live under conditions of oppressive security, on a gated estate or in a house with intricate alarm systems and maybe a bodyguard or two. But if you are sufficiently well known that a nomadic Mongolian horse herder can meet you and categorically declare that no, you are not who you say you are, because in person you are quite unlike the image of who you say you are that he carries around in his head, that is fame of a completely different order.

One could easily dismiss Henmedeh's assumption as a simple error made by an unsophisticated man unused to meeting global celebrities. One could, if Julia Roberts herself did not provide evidence that her encounters with fans in the West were not equally peculiar and confused. She has strong opinions about her fame and the sheer weirdness that sometimes surrounds it. And one afternoon, on a break from shooting the 1999 film *Notting Hill* (in a self-reflecting role, Roberts, the world's most famous movie actress, was playing the world's most famous movie actress) she mused on the more unsettling aspects of what it means to be a global celebrity today.

'You go to a dinner party and meet people, and say "Hi, I'm Julia,"' she recounted. 'And people will say, "Oh, I know who you are." If there were any way not to sound rude, I'd say, "You think you do, but you don't really, so why don't we start right here and go from there." They've seen you go through these trials and tribulations in movies, and for them you become that person. It's hard for some people to let that go. They feel this is information they have about you. They'll recite to me the plot of one of my films, *My Best Friend's Wedding*, say, and they think what happened in that film has happened to me. It's hard to make people understand that no, you don't really know me. You think you do, and I don't hold it against you, but you really don't. It's bizarre. It's an interesting conundrum.'

Julia Roberts experiences fame to a degree shared by few other people. I had been about to write that she enjoys fame, yet 'enjoys' is clearly not the right word. How disoriented and distorted must the world seem to her, when so much about her life and personality is assumed and pre-judged in this manner? But then it is a sobering fact that when modern-day fame comes crashing into the life of someone hitherto obscure, the consequences are complex.

I have spent much of the past twenty years, mainly in Britain and the United States, meeting, talking to and writing about famous people, most of them in one branch or another of the entertainment industry. As has frequently been pointed out to me, this is not a terrible way to make a living, and it has placed me in intriguing situations.

I once spent an afternoon alone with Fred Astaire in his Beverly Hills mansion. At one point he stood and demonstrated a few steps of a soft-shoe shuffle, beaming with delight. Later on, he sat down at his piano and sang Irving Berlin's 'Isn't This A Lovely Day?'. So Astaire has sung and danced for me, an audience of one. I spent days on end in Cracow, Poland, standing at the shoulder of Steven Spielberg as he directed scenes from his Holocaust film *Schindler's List*, listening as he explained why he formulated a particular shot in a certain way. Occasionally he would ask me what I thought of his choices, nodding seriously when I told him, as though my opinions were of value.

Late in 1991, I found myself tiptoeing around two cavernous rooms inside the Kremlin, desperately trying to make no noise as I watched a small cast and crew race against the clock to shoot scenes for a TV movie about the life of Josef Stalin, starring Robert Duvall as the murderous dictator. One floor below us, Mikhail Gorbachev was conducting solemn state business – the reason the film crew had to be as swift and discreet as possible.

During that stay in Moscow, I stayed in a remote, cavernous dacha twelve miles outside the city that had been Stalin's personal retreat; the film production company commandeered it for a couple of weeks, and shot scenes in its extensive wooded grounds. The dacha had been out of use since Stalin's death forty years previously, but a small staff kept it in immaculate condition, as if the old tyrant might stride through its doors again at any moment. It stood as a monument to his mounting paranoia in his later years; a secret underground railway linked it to the Kremlin so that he might travel to central Moscow without the threat of being seen and attacked by assassins. This was a real fear. A prisoner of the fame he had so assiduously created for himself, Stalin finally trusted no one. Doctors were terrified at being summoned to treat him even for minor maladies; he was liable to accuse them of trying to kill him with medication, and order them to be executed. That week, I actually slept in Stalin's bed. But then lots of beds in the dacha were Stalin's; near the end of his life he would rotate the rooms he slept in, to foil the unseen killers he imagined must be lurking outside.

In a high, softly-lit room in a mountaintop Los Angeles home with central American religious art lining its walls, giving it the appearance of a Mexican cathedral, a heavily pregnant Madonna and I once spent a couple of hours sitting close together at right angles on high, throne-like chairs upholstered in red plush velvet. Madonna's extraordinary outfit of a diaphanous black dress over a transparent body stocking only served to accentuate her distended belly; ironically, she talked that afternoon of, among other things, self-exposure, the need to impose limits on it, and the struggle to retain some sense of a private self, even if you are the world's best-known pop icon.

I have lost count of the number of truly famous people I have encountered, though it easily runs into hundreds. I have met them in their homes, in restaurants and cafes. I have talked to them in TV studios, in luxurious but impersonal hotel rooms paid for by a TV network, a film studio or a record company. I have listened to them in large air-conditioned trailers on film locations, beside their swimming pools, and in the back of chauffeured limousines.

I have talked and listened, but I have also watched. I know the routine when a celebrity walks towards a group of lowly crew people on a film set; without a word needing to be spoken between them, they part like the Red Sea to let the celebrity through. When a famous person enters a restaurant, sits down and orders a meal, much of the conversation in the immediate area effectively grinds to a halt. Onlookers tend to become distracted from what is going on at their own tables, and find their gaze almost involuntarily drifting towards the celebrity and his table companions; they may soon find themselves confirming in hushed whispers what dressing he has selected for his salad. I know what happens when famous people walk into crowded rooms. The light seems to waft in their direction; the very molecules in the air seem to rearrange themselves. Their smallest whim is swiftly accommodated; if they want to smoke or drink, fingers snap, gestures of exaggerated urgency are made, and a lighter or a full glass will appear.

I have seen all of these things repeatedly. Yet something I have rarely if ever heard is a request by a celebrity being met by the simple word 'no', a negotiation that the non-famous among us experience on a daily basis. There is a reason for this, of course. When people acquire fame, they also often acquire retinues, a raft of assistants and handlers whose sole job it is to keep them happy – or, put more accurately, to acquiesce to their every stated wish. This boundless desire to comply has an economic basis; they are employees who need to hang on to their jobs. But celebrities represent a financial wellspring to people far beyond their own retinues. In the entertainment industry, for instance, executives from a film studio, a record company or a TV network, have sound business reasons for appeasing stars' whims, justifiably fearing they may otherwise offer their valuable services to commercial rivals. The cycle of acquiescence thus goes on; instead of the taboo word 'no', a desperate series of increasingly attractive alternative offers is made until an uneasy agreement is reached.

When you spend long enough observing the famous, several questions eventually begin to form. What must it be like to have people scurrying around, trying to meet your every desire? What does it feel like not to have to meet the minimum standards of courtesy and tolerance routinely demanded of non-famous people, but instead to have your petulance, rudeness and impatience ignored and forgiven? What does it do to the psyche to move between personal interactions in which everyone else knows who you are (or as Julia Roberts would insist, thinks they do) and yet you know only a small minority of others? Can one hang on to one's sense of self when most other people are going out of their way to fulfil your wishes, without any corresponding obligation from you?

Few of us are so saintly not to admit that, for a time at least, it would be a tempting proposition. Who would not like to be the centre of attention, to experience one's desires being constantly accommodated? Would it not be agreeable to have everyone you meet laugh uproariously at your witticisms, and to be able to command and redirect the conversation of others with the smallest gesture? Does it not sound appealing to have your every comment on the most trivial topics reported by the media to a global audience? Who could resist the prospect of being best-friend material to one's own gender, and an object of sexual fantasy to everyone else? Who could resist the lure of the flashbulbs and the smiles and the applause? Who, in short, would not desire fame?

It certainly holds a superficial allure for many of us; the trappings of celebrity can look like a career structure in themselves. Young people, asked what they want to be as adults, sometimes reply, 'Famous', with not a single thought to what kind of endeavour it might be attached. And in fairness, why should they think differently? Ours is an age in which fame no longer necessarily depends on achievement; our TV screens, newspapers and magazines are filled as never before with people who seem famous just for being famous. (The American historian Daniel Boorstin first coined this idea: 'A celebrity is a person who is well known for his well-knownness.')

Still, if fame has become democratized, appears easier than ever to attain, and looks like a viable job option in its own right, it is not something to embark upon frivolously. The impact of fame, and especially sudden or early fame, cannot be prepared for from obscurity, and its side-effects can be disorienting. Each advantage of celebrity in terms of material gain or outer show carries a down side, sometimes unseen but often of equal weight. Fame often arrives accompanied by new wealth, which can be welcome. But alongside that wealth may come a sense of personal intrusion – being constantly recognized and approached in public, seeing the details of one's private life relentlessly picked over and discussed by the media. Soon a sense of personal freedom previously taken for granted can seem curtailed. Fame may bring widespread approbation and applause. But it is of a peculiarly generalized kind, coming as it does from a large audience, few of whom know the famous person intimately; all they know is an image of someone, constructed selectively and calculatingly for public dissemination.

Those growing up with ambitions to be famous often assume they would attain happiness from basking in the glow of such public adoration. When it happens, they often find it less fulfilling and more impersonal than they expected. Instead, the disparity between their real personality and the selective image held up for public consumption can induce self-doubt. They may start to feel inadequate. They may worry they are impostors, presenting a false face to an audience led to revere them under false pretences. Fame may elevate a person from humble origins into the loftier echelons of society, a factor that is part of its allure. Yet even this effect has drawbacks, especially when fame arrives suddenly. New celebrities tend to be thrust into new environments, where they find themselves surrounded by people unfamiliar to them but whose job it is to arrange their lives. Typically, they have more disposable income and far more demands on their time. Psychologically, this can be jarring and disorienting; it is akin to assuming a fresh identity without quite shedding the old one. There is often a need to re-align relationships with their family, and with friends and acquaintances from their obscure past. How do newly famous people behave when they return to their old haunts? As if their fame had never happened? Should they talk enthusiastically about their glittering new life? They could come across as overbearing. If sudden wealth is involved, another problem arises: do they make a show of generosity to their family and friends, and risk the charge of seeming patronizing? Or do they act as if their financial situation were unaltered? That might be construed as miserly.

Fame to non-celebrities and, specifically, would-be celebrities may look like an absolute condition: you're famous or you're not, but once attained, it's permanent. In fact, fame may be transient in the extreme, notwithstanding the best-known popular song on the subject, 'Fame', from the hit 1980 film of the same name. It proclaims, with poignant wishful thinking: 'I'm gonna live forever/Baby remember my name'. The cast played a bunch of young hopefuls at a performing arts school in New York; but in real life, not one actor in the film or its spinoff TV series found long-lasting fame, or anything like it. Even Irene Cara, who had a big hit with the song, is now recalled only as an ironic trivia item, in terms of her subsequent non-fame.

In Los Angeles and New York City one can find thousands of actors who appeared briefly in short-lived, long-forgotten TV series, and thousands more musicians who were in pop groups that enjoyed a single minor hit but never repeated the trick. These people gamely stick around town, attending auditions, hoping vainly that fame's lightning bolt will strike a second time. But they are outnumbered by thousands more wannabes, younger, hungrier and less jaded, among whose ranks tomorrow's briefly famous are more likely to be found. Most people today who attain any measure of fame do so for a short period – Andy Warhol's metaphorical fifteen minutes. And what happens to them after that?

Clearly, then, fame is a complicated phenomenon, one with as many downfalls as advantages. Yet one would never surmise this from the state of the media at the beginning of the twenty-first century. Television, magazines and newspapers are now overwhelmingly committed to propagating the notion that fame, in all its variations, is a hugely desirable end in itself. Of course television, magazines and newspapers are businesses, reliant on high audience ratings or healthy circulations for revenue and advertising income. And famous people 'sell' a media product with unparalleled efficiency. To adopt a more critical view towards fame might constitute rocking the very principles upon which modern media are predicated. To go further and question why ordinary people seem to need to know the intricate details of famous people's lives would be tantamount to media heresy. It would be another way of asking: why are you watching or reading this nonsense? Even so, the extent to which television and the print media airbrush out of existence the inconveniently complex and undesirable side-effects of fame is intriguing to behold. For print interviews, the famous are usually photographed to make them look as attractive as possible. The image that appears may already have been approved by their publicity handlers as a pre-condition for the media to be granted access to them in the first place. Often, what journalists are allowed to ask them is agreed in advance, thus avoiding contentious or embarrassing areas of conversation. The text surrounding the flattering pictures may itself have been tampered with: celebrities frequently request and sometimes receive 'copy approval', which means that a vigilant publicist in their employ has the right to inspect it and blue-pencil any quote, comment or observation by the journalist deemed negative or unhelpful to the star's interests. Again, this is a price sections of the media often pay for access to celebrities.

What remains is a form of low-level propaganda – a calculatedly partial profile of a human personality, minus any aspects that might dilute the message, irritate the celebrity, or simply be bad for business. Modesty, wit, tolerance, grace, self-effacement, good humour and a social conscience: these are usually among the qualities media exposure seeks to invoke – plus unbridled enthusiasm for the film, TV show, record, book or whatever the celebrity is plugging. (No wonder that the celebrity, reading the enhanced 'truth' about himself and comparing it with his private doubts about himself on an average day, can end up feeling confused and alienated by the processes of fame.) All this convoluted engineering of the truth has the one aim of enhancing the 'brand' that the famous person has become, both in financial and cultural terms. And the end result is something the media find convenient and profitable in our self-absorbed age: the assertion of the individual.

Few areas of public discourse or human endeavour have not been distorted in recent years to accommodate a media viewpoint that emphasizes the personalities of individuals over the detailed substance of issues. This has long been true of the entertainment industry, as one might expect. But it is now equally true of sport, politics, business, literature and science; the prevailing tendency is to reduce all areas of life to their 'human interest' and entertainment value.

For example, one might have thought theoretical physics invulnerable to such a tendency. But in the unlikely figure of Stephen Hawking, theoretical physics now has a human face. Hawking, of course, is a good story. As a brilliant young research student in his early twenties, he was diagnosed with the disabling condition motor neurone disease. (One might have thought motor neurone disease equally invulnerable to the tendency, but think again: it is also known as Lou Gehrig's disease, after the baseball player who contracted it.) Confined to a wheelchair, Hawking has bodily control only in his left hand. He needs nursing care round the clock, and communicates by clicking on a mouse that inputs conversation to a computer on his wheelchair.

In 1988, his book *A Brief History of Time*, which sets out to impose some underlying order on the universe through his exploration of big bangs and black holes, became a publishing phenomenon. It sold some 10 million copies, was translated into forty languages, and remained on best-seller lists worldwide for years. It hardly mattered that lay readers struggled mightily to understand it, even though Hawking deliberately wrote the book without recourse to mathematical equations; *A Brief History of Time* remains one of the great all-time best-sellers largely unfinished by its readers. Hawking soon became famous, the best-known scientific mind since Albert Einstein. The media had a field day; fawning articles on him rarely failed to point out that here was an extraordinary, agile brain ticking over in an inert, pathetically dependent body. People who didn't know a quark from a black hole were fascinated by the poignant paradox.

He even became the star of his own movie, a stylized documentary produced by Steven Spielberg no less, also titled *A Brief History Of Time*. Shooting it largely required wheeling Hawking into a studio, where he sat motionless in front of blue screens, on which the director later superimposed images of mathematical formulae and pictures of outer space. Hawking, who is not a man lacking in ego, happily participated in the film as a plausible project that might enhance his fame. He instinctively grasped that role-playing is an essential component of celebrity. 'I fit the part of a disabled genius,' he told me. 'At least, I'm disabled – even though I'm not a genius like Einstein.' Later, he said: 'The public wants heroes. They made Einstein a hero, and now they are making me one. Though with much less justification.' (He invariably played down his gifts with self-effacing disclaimers, even while constantly bracketing himself with Einstein.)

This was about as far as his story as a famous person could go. Yes, he was a disabled genius, firstly by being one, and secondly by submitting himself to a process allowing him to be widely recognized as one. But he was hardly a contender for long-term fame. Hawking has a dry wit, and could answer questions in droll fashion, but it took time for him to input them into his computer, so his answers emerged rather lamely after some two minutes. To put it mildly, this made him less than ideal material for TV talk shows. If one had read (or tried to read) his book, and seen the film (which also turned out to be forbiddingly heavy going), there was no obvious direction in which his fame could further flourish.

Until, that is, his domestic arrangements became public. He separated from Jane, his wife of twenty-five years who had known him since before his terrible illness, and took up with Elaine Mason, his primary nurse and carer. Finally, the media had something else to say about Hawking. They seized upon his marital break-up with something approaching glee, never pausing to sympathize about the pressures and stress behind holding together a marriage overshadowed by such debilitating illness in the first place. Hawking had nothing to say publicly about the media coverage, but one can imagine he must have been stunned. With *A Brief History of Time* he had shown himself susceptible to the lure of fame; he contracted it as if it were a virus. Like others before him who embarked on the process of self-aggrandizement involved in letting yourself become famous, he was content for his celebrity status to be advanced on his own terms.

But he failed to understand two conditions that always attach themselves to fame. The first is that fame resembles a spring-loaded door that slams behind you after you walk through it. Once you invite the media (and by extension the world) into what magazines such as *Hello!* and *OK!* routinely call your 'lovely home', and invite them to peruse your decor, soft furnishings, possessions, wealth, romantic relationships, children and pets, there is no turning back. No matter that your motives for inviting them initially were lofty. No matter that you only did it because a new book, film or record had to be publicized. They will return whenever the occasion warrants, invited or not.

And that leads to the second condition attached to fame: continuing celebrity is a form of narrative, in which achieving fame is just the first chapter. Once people are established celebrities, the media reports things about them that are irrelevant to what first made them famous. If a nonentity is found face down and drunk in a gutter, few will care. But a similar fall from grace by a celebrity is a big story, and the fact he may be a Nobel prize winner will not mitigate the offence, nor temper the mercilessness of the reporting. Celebrity carries with it an odd moral neutrality, and the innocence with which people succumb to the fame virus counts for nothing; once they are famous, their every false move is ruthlessly scrutinized. If they crash a car, argue publicly with a spouse, are seen leaving a massage parlour, display temper, impatience or inappropriate grandeur, or even under-tip a waiter, they should assume the media may record the fact.

This is the ugly flipside of fame that the non-famous rarely pause to consider. Unsurprisingly, it is largely unreported; the media, after all, have a vested commercial interest in propagating the notion that fame is an entirely good thing. It is hard to agree. It may be a generalization of a necessarily unscientific kind, but the famous people I meet seem as a group less well adjusted and more ill-at-ease than the norm. Strikingly guarded and defensive, they are more liable to perceive a slight where none exists. Small inconveniences or mishaps that most people might easily shrug aside often unsettle them disproportionately. They are not a notably happy breed. Psychologically, the condition of fame has corrosive elements; it can engender distrust and isolation, and has a potential to play havoc with one's sense of identity and self-worth. Western society endorses fame with the indirectly stated promise that, once it is attained, it may solve all kinds of personal problems; yet many famous people find it empty and anti-climactic.

So who needs fame? Everyone who has ever had aspirations to rise above the herd and carve out individual achievements, of course. The impulse to be famous looks to be an innate human instinct, a striving to follow wherever one's gifts may lead. Cynics might rightly observe that this same impulse has given us Hitler, Stalin, Mao Tse-tung and any number of serial killers. True – but it has also given us Shakespeare, Keats, Marie Curie and Nelson Mandela. The diversity of the consequences does not detract from the original conviction and authenticity of the impulse.

A book arguing against humankind's aspirations towards fame would be a forlorn undertaking. Yet the nature of modern fame has altered so drastically in recent years, in ways that can weigh heavily against people in the public eye, that its less apparent disadvantages are well worth exploring. It's as good a place as any to begin.

2

Fame Becomes a Problem

RULE TWO:
In fame's wake, lives get ruined – and sometimes prematurely ended

Fame used to be a relatively simple matter. One could achieve it in a limited number of ways: ruling a nation, conquering other nations by leading armies into battle, discovering lost continents, making significant scientific discoveries. For thousands of years, fame rarely seemed to be a problem for the famous; it did not tend to rebound in a negative manner on their lives. News of their exploits was transmitted with their blessing, in ways unseen and often unknown to them. Cave paintings are probably the oldest medium for passing on the deeds of the celebrated, and only then to a limited audience. But in the pre-printing age, oral histories, sagas and epics, sometimes relayed to whole communities at a single sitting, did the job. The famous could live on in the collective memory through statues, coins, gigantic tombs (the Pyramids being only the most spectacular example) and by having their bodies mummified. From their point of view, it was a benign by-product of their achievements.

They even had the advantage that they could see fame coming. It used to be something you accumulated gradually. It was something you could prepare for. The world had to wait until March 1812 until a celebrity had anything to say about the condition of fame that sounded remotely modern. This was Lord Byron, reacting to the instant success of the first two cantos of his poem *Childe Harold's Pilgrimage*. 'I awoke one morning and found myself famous,' he wrote, thus certifying himself as the first overnight sensation.

Byron is an intriguing figure in fame's history for another reason. He unwittingly created a template for a certain kind of celebrity, a disaffected, pouting, sexually alluring young man who rails at the shortcomings of older generations and makes great play of being perpetually misunderstood. Echoes of his fame can be found in dozens of subsequent figures: F. Scott Fitzgerald, Marlon Brando, James Dean, Jack Kerouac, Mick Jagger, Jim Morrison, all the way up to Kurt Cobain and Eminem. Had Byron set out to invent his autobiography as a Romantic construct, it could scarcely have been more potent than the facts of his real life. He had a club foot, and was sensitive about it; he had a history of sexual ambivalence; he enjoyed such a surfeit of revelry and pleasure that he wearied of it, and said so; he embarked on affairs with society women; and crucially, he died at the appallingly early age of thirty-six. His is a tough legend to follow.

Byron's was not the sort of fame that found him being mobbed in the streets. He was hugely famous in the society circles he frequented, and among the Whigs with whom he sat in the House of Lords. But the young women who avidly read each page of *Childe Harold's Pilgrimage* with a longing for the young Byron in their hearts had little idea of what he really looked like.

Nineteenth-century fame was easier in that regard, and David Livingstone was another good example. The great explorer-missionary had been a famous figure in Britain since his mid-thirties, when he discovered Lake Ngami. But with each successive expedition into the African heartland, his fame increased; his explorations of the Zambezi culminated in his discovery of what he patriotically named Victoria Falls, after his queen. Throughout the Empire, and indeed the English-speaking world, Livingstone was a hero. On his return in 1856, he wrote a volume about his explorations, *Missionary Travels and Researches in South Africa*, which became an immediate best-seller, and finally made him wealthy. He embarked on a six-month speaking tour of Britain. Still, few who did not turn up to hear him had much idea of what he looked like in the flesh.

Now consider the famous quote that bears his name, 'Dr Livingstone, I presume.' It was said to him in 1871 by Henry Morton Stanley, a journalist charged by his newspaper, the *New York Herald*, to find Livingstone, who had gone missing on his long expedition to trace the source of the Nile. Stanley finally cornered his ailing prey at a point deeper into central Africa than any European had previously ventured. Did Stanley know in advance what Livingstone looked like? Whether he did or not, his was a greeting to a celebrity that now sounds almost courtly: try saying 'Bill Clinton, I presume', or 'Nelson Mandela, I presume', or 'Madonna, I presume' straight-faced. Stanley's circumspection suggests that even a man as famous as Livingstone could go about his life without suffering intrusion.

At least Livingstone had done something – several things, in fact – to justify his fame. The concept of fame as we understand it now would have been hard to grasp until almost a hundred years ago. For centuries fame was linked strictly to position or achievement, and no one became famous beyond the measure of their accomplishments. Nor was it a matter that involved the unpleasantness of personal interference; monarchs might visit small towns in their kingdoms, but their subjects lining the streets to see them knew their place and kept a respectful distance.

Around 1900, two events began to change all this: moving pictures became available to the public, and a genuinely popular press emerged. What united these events was that both industries in their early days grasped the need to invent celebrities to advance their expansion.

Alfred Charles Harmsworth, later Lord Northcliffe, founded Britain's first popular newspaper, the *Daily Mail*, in 1896. Sensing huge profits could be made in entertaining readers rather than providing a public service, he set himself against a tradition of papers with long, dull stories in long, dull columns. Aiming at the middle classes, the *Mail* reflected in its pages the topics its readers might discuss or gossip about in their everyday lives. He downplayed reports about matters of state, foreign policy and economic questions, and instead gave prominence to sensationalist accounts of crime – murders in juicy detail, confession letters printed in full, and the like.

Northcliffe printed stories in serial form and published household hints, to attract women readers. The *Mail* triumphed in Britain's military successes abroad, and its circulation sky-rocketed during the Boer War. It took on populist campaigns, and adopted a cavalier attitude towards facts, simply mixing them with opinion. This emphasis on entertainment paid off; by 1921, the paper was selling a remarkable 1.5 million daily.

The *Daily Express*, owned by the Canadian William Maxwell Aitken, later Lord Beaverbrook, took this process a stage further. One of his big ideas was peopling its pages with a cast of colourful real-life characters. Many seemed to be dotty, faintly aristocratic eccentrics, but they provided running narratives for curious readers. There was Lady Dorothy Mills, a travel writer who lived for a month among Liberian cannibals, but survived to tell *Express* readers her story. (She was apparently in little danger, as women were regarded as having less tender flesh than men.) A Mrs Smith-Wilkinson from Matlock, Derbyshire was so profligate she was nicknamed 'The Countess of Monte Cristo'; in 1923 she allegedly spent £30,000 on a clothes shopping spree in London, while keeping her husband Edward in penury, paying him eight shillings a week. Readers were riveted by these new celebrities, and by 1937 the *Express* had the world's biggest circulation, 2.5 million.

The emergence of the popular press in America was also dominated by two media magnates, Joseph Pulitzer and William Randolph Hearst. Pulitzer, whose name today has only dignified associations through the journalism and cultural prizes bearing his name, was viewed as more disreputable in his time. In 1883 he transformed the *New York World* into a sensationalist newspaper complete with screaming, breathless headlines about terrible crimes and awful natural disasters. He made the paper more visually striking through the use of cartoons, illustrations and comic strips. He even printed banner headlines in red ink to underline their effect.

In 1895 Hearst bought a rival newspaper, the *New York Journal*, and set his sights at Pulitzer's *World*. An editorial from its early days set out his philosophy: 'The public is even more fond of entertainment than it is of information.' And entertainment was what Hearst offered. Other newspaper owners had found that the news was often not exciting enough, but he was the first to solve the problem by reworking it into a more exciting form of itself. The *Journal* included the feature News Novelettes From Real Life, written by a desk-bound editor using material garnered from the day's news wires. These were scrutinized, then rewritten, sometimes past the point of recognition, for maximum dramatic effect.

On a grander scale Hearst, through his *Journal*, agitated successfully for the US to declare war against Spain in 1898. His motives were breathtakingly uncomplicated: like Northcliffe, he saw wars as potential circulation boosters. He sent echelons of reporters to Cuba to seek out civil unrest, and was impatient if they found little evidence of it. When the artist Frederic Remington wired Hearst that Havana was quiet, Hearst reportedly wired back, 'You furnish the pictures and I will furnish the war.'

Apart from massaging the facts, Hearst knew the value of fame and celebrity. He encouraged journalists to insert themselves into their own reports, sharing with readers the ways in which they virtuously revealed injustice and wrongdoing. In doing this, of course, his journalists embodied entertainment values – creating stories in which they had the starring roles.

Newspapers in both Britain and the US were learning new tricks that might pave the way to mass circulation. Readers preferred being entertained to being lectured. They wanted to read about individuals rather than abstract ideas, and they were thirsty for celebrities, whether their fame was rooted in solid achievement or manufactured by the newspaper itself. These celebrities could even be hand-picked for infamy; Fred Ebb and Bob Fosse's musical *Chicago* brilliantly satirizes how American papers in the 1920s feverishly competed to find a glamorous female 'murderer of the week'.

The film industry learned the value of stars, and of publicizing them, even more quickly. In America theatrical exhibition of films was barely a decade old when Florence Lawrence emerged as a major screen presence. In 1907 she had joined Biograph Films and enjoyed a meteoric rise, starring in some of D. W. Griffith's earliest efforts. But for a while her identity was unknown. Biograph had a policy of not promoting actors by name, fearing they would feel emboldened to ask for more money. But because Florence Lawrence was such a natural on screen, the selfless company coined a name for her and she became known as the Biograph Girl.

This did not last long. In the first inter-studio coup of its kind, the film pioneer Carl Laemmle lured her from Biograph in 1910, signing her to his Independent Motion Picture Company of America, widely known as IMP, whereupon Lawrence assumed a new name, the IMP Girl. Laemmle now engineered a public relations stunt, anonymously fabricating a newspaper story that she had been killed in a streetcar accident. He then took out an advertisement, complaining that enemies of IMP had spread rumours of her death. In fact, he added happily, the reverse was true: Florence Lawrence was alive and well, and would be starring in IMP's next big production, *The Broken Oath*. This magnificent piece of chicanery not only hyped Laemmle's acquisition of Lawrence, but also reassured a worried public about her well-being and publicized her upcoming IMP picture. Historically, it was more significant: it made her the first American film star known by her own name.

Laemmle's shameless stunt proved to the early motion picture industry that it was possible to create a stir of interest, even a nationwide sensation, around a film and its stars without reference to its worth or their talent. He was not the first American entrepreneur to realize the commercial possibilities of trumpeting hype rather than substance. In this respect, Laemmle was following in the tradition of Phineas T. Barnum, whose flair for exaggerated, sensational publicity turned the American circus into The Greatest Show on Earth. Barnum dreamed up his first PR scam as early as 1835, when he presented to the public Joice Heth, a very elderly black woman who he claimed was George Washington's 160-year-old nurse. By the time his hoax was rumbled, Barnum was off on his next project.

Laemmle and his fellow studio bosses adopted the cavalier spirit in which Barnum hyped his acts, and institutionalized it. The studios were not only in the business of creating movies; each had a publicity division devoted to creating stars. Just as in Highland Park, Michigan, Henry Ford's Model Ts began rolling off newly-developed assembly lines in their thousands, starting around 1913, so the concept of mass production began to be applied to movie stars. The entertainment business became the first industry to treat the creation of fame as if it were an industrial process. In their early days, film studios invented mechanisms for churning out charismatic, desirable new stars at regular intervals, as if from an assembly line. The studio bosses played a hunch that the public could tolerate the prospect of a whole lot more famous people in the world, and their gamble paid off beyond even their expansive imaginations.

After the Florence Lawrence breakthrough, new movie stars began to emerge rapidly: Mary Pickford, Lillian Gish and her sister Dorothy, Fatty Arbuckle, Douglas Fairbanks, Harold Lloyd, Buster Keaton –

and above all Charlie Chaplin, soon to become arguably the world's most famous man. But initially Pickford was the one who most successfully exploited her own celebrity, and used it to gain financial clout and creative muscle. She began her film career in 1909 at Biograph, where she was known simply as Little Mary or The Girl With The Golden Hair, at a salary of $40 a week. She moved to IMP the following year for $175 a week, and the year after that to Majestic for $275. In 1912 she signed to Adolph Zukor's Famous Players Company for $500 a week, and it seemed that each year her pay rose dramatically. In 1916, she renewed her contract with Zukor for $10,000 a week, in addition to a signing-on bonus of $300,000. There was an extra inducement when she was allowed to start The Mary Pickford Company, an affiliate devoted exclusively to producing films for her to star in.

But even that was not enough. In 1917 she moved to First National for $350,000 a movie, and in 1919, she declared complete independence from the studio system, founding United Artists with two other actors and a director, Chaplin, Fairbanks and D. W. Griffith.

Yet for all Pickford's astuteness, Chaplin's rise was the more remarkable. Born into poverty in London, where he and his brother Sydney had stage careers with the Fred Karno comedy troupe, he moved to America and joined Mack Sennett's Keystone production company in 1913. In his year at Keystone, he appeared in thirty-five films, some of which he also wrote and directed. Around this time, Chaplin began to formulate in various films the character that would make him world-famous, the resilient, heroic Little Tramp who overcomes the most daunting of odds. In 1915, this character came to full flower in the film *The Tramp*, and Chaplin's career went into orbit. In the next three years he became a huge international celebrity. By the time he jointly founded United Artists, he had been making films for less than six years. A decade earlier, no actor was even credited by name; now three of them were running their own studio.

Why did the movies come to exert such huge influence on the history of fame? Almost solely because of a single cinematic technique – the close-up. For the first time one could see a moving image of a face, thirty feet high, and that fact had all sorts of consequences. An audience could see the most minute tic on a star's face, and could discern emotion in the flicker of a giant projected eyelid. There was a new, visceral strangeness in seeing another's face up close and personal, and being able to inspect it at one's leisure. In their own lives, the only time audiences ever got to do this was with a lover or sexual partner. Thus the close-up immediately gave them an illusion of intimacy with stars, in a way they had never been able to achieve with distant actors on a theatre stage, or the sort of famous people they merely read about in newspapers or magazines. Inevitably, the audience started to convince themselves they had a relationship with these stars. They began to speculate freely about their lives off-screen, their whims, preferences and real-life characteristics.

Pickford and Fairbanks, who married in 1920, became, with Chaplin, the first exemplars of Hollywood celebrity. To say they were unprepared for it would be to understate the case. Notoriety attended Chaplin from his first experiences with fame. During World War I, he was savagely criticized in Britain for not returning home to serve in the armed forces, when in fact he had been rejected on medical grounds. His weakness for adolescent girls was also the subject of caustic comment. In 1918, aged twenty-nine, he married for the first time; his bride was sixteen-year-old film extra Mildred Harris. During his lifetime, Chaplin was to marry four women still in their teens.

Pickford and Fairbanks never suffered such opprobrium; she, after all, was universally known as America's Sweetheart. They bought a magnificent villa in expansive grounds high on a promontory above Sunset Boulevard in Beverly Hills. They named it Pickfair, and it became an informal court for Hollywood's new aristocracy – or at least its highest earners. And Doug and Mary were the town's *de facto* monarchs.

Everything was under control for as long as they stayed in what looked to the outside world like a magical kingdom. Their problems arose when they ventured outside. Visiting Europe on their honeymoon, they saw at first hand what a dual-edged proposition fame could be. This dashing, glamorous couple were mobbed wherever they went. They were almost trampled underfoot en route to a garden party in London; in Paris, the sheer number of people straining for a glimpse of them made them fear for their lives. Their safety was being jeopardized by the very fans who professed to adore them. Fairbanks seemed to take it largely in his stride, but Pickford became horrified by her fame. Her fans might still have perceived her as the sweet little girl with a curl, though she was now thirty years old. But in private she was shy, reclusive – and no stranger to the pleasures of alcohol. The mob scenes that greeted her and her new husband in Europe were not what she expected, and being confronted by her own fame in such a stark manner was something she never learned to cope with.

The new generation of celebrities had also failed to take account of the fact that the media were changing their outlook. It had once been the case that reporters showed a proper deference towards everyone anointed with the status of fame. Now, celebrities were viewed merely as vehicles for sensational, circulation-grabbing stories, and their sensitivities were of no importance. Stories could portray them in a flattering or an unflattering light; either way, they were useful for the papers' circulation drives. The potential consequences for Hollywood were dire. If stars received bad publicity, or newspapers started rabble-rousing campaigns against them, their careers could be jeopardized. And that was bad for business.

It did not take long before the career of one of Hollywood's earliest stars was sacrificed on the altar of public outrage. Fatty Arbuckle was at the peak of his success; after making many short comedies with Sennett's Keystone Cops, he set up his own production company. In 1921 he threw a wild party at a San Francisco hotel where a starlet, Virginia Rapp, was seized by convulsions, and died a few days later of a ruptured bladder. Accused of sexually assaulting her, Arbuckle stood trial for manslaughter. The case ended twice with a hung jury; third time around, he was acquitted. But the press fuelled the scandal, public disgust seemed genuine, and the fledgling movie industry became a byword for libertinism and vice. The industry closed ranks, setting up the Hays Office to censor films and regulate the behaviour of its own employees. Arbuckle's films were banned and he never worked again as an actor.

Despite Arbuckle's disgrace (this, of course, was before celebrities employed spin doctors to 'manage' their fame and reposition their foibles and misdeeds in the most positive light), few denied that <u>sex was an integral part of the new Hollywood stars' appeal</u>. Fairbanks had become famous not because of his devotion to his acting craft, but

FAME BECOMES A PROBLEM

because millions of young women entertained erotic fantasies about him. Among actresses, the obvious example was Clara Bow, who launched her career by winning a prize in a beauty contest sponsored by a magazine for film fans. The prize was a bit part in a movie. When she joined Paramount (under the tutelage of its new staff producer B. P. Schulberg, crucially a former publicity director at another studio) the studio's PR machine went into overdrive, and Bow was reinvented, with bobbed hair, dramatic eye make-up and lips shaped like a Cupid's bow. She swiftly emerged as an icon of the 1920s – a sparky little flapper, vivacious, liberated, and above all sexually desirable.

She and the 1927 film *It* were waiting to happen to each other, and it hardly mattered that the film was nothing special. Bow was dazzling as a flirtatious, ambitious department store salesgirl with very obvious designs on her dashing boss. Thereafter Bow was universally known as the It Girl, and everyone knew what It meant: in the phrase of the film's screenwriter Elinor Glyn, It was 'a strange magnetism which attracts both sexes'.

For a short period, Bow was very famous indeed as the purveyor of a sex appeal that one might term naughty but nice. The fascination of *It* spilled over to encompass Glyn, an Englishwoman best known for faintly outrageous novels, which caused a sensation in their time but did not sell widely enough to keep her out of debt. She moved to Hollywood in 1920, and cultivated the company of the rich and famous, like Chaplin and Hearst. Her script for *It* made her a minor celebrity with a reputation for fast living, and she was immortalized in a short poem by Ogden Nash, which racily rhymed 'sin' and 'tiger skin' with 'Elinor Glyn'.

All this was rather harmless and innocent. However, the Hays Office was looming in the wings, bursting with moralistic notions of what could and could not be portrayed in 'decent' movies; in 1930 it issued a Motion Picture Production Code, and ordered the studios to regulate themselves. When it turned out that the delectable Clara Bow's private life was tinged with sexual scandal, the public mood turned against her. She suffered a series of nervous breakdowns, and faded from view as quickly as she had emerged, making her last film in 1933.

Clearly this fame business needed to be handled with care. Unspoken parameters were coming into play, lines were being drawn that a celebrity simply could not cross. Arbuckle's conduct obviously fell outside what was deemed acceptable by the public, the media and his own industry. As for Chaplin, he spent his whole career in a kind of protracted public negotiation about his own suitability as a star, mostly centred round his teenage brides or girlfriends, and his outspoken left-wing politics. For many years, he was suspected of subversive activities, and remained under heavy surveillance from the FBI. Widely criticized in America for advocating a Second Front against Nazi Germany in 1942, he was finally barred from the United States in 1952, and settled in Switzerland. But he emerged from exile in 1972 to accept an honorary Oscar from a wildly applauding Academy.

By the early 1920s, the battle lines had effectively been drawn. How much of themselves should famous people be prepared to share with their public? What areas of life should remain hidden away? How should they conduct themselves in public and private? And even if their conduct remained impeccable, how should they define their relationship with their fans? Should they reciprocate their warmth, desired intimacy and friendship? Or did it make better sense to remain aloof, hoping that their manner and body language defused more extreme expressions of adulation? No one had a definitive answer; these new celebrities were traversing virgin terrain.

Such problems were by no means restricted to people in the entertainment industry. T. E. Lawrence achieved a kind of fame comparable to the new movie stars through his exploits in the Middle East; he helped foment the Arab uprising against the Turks, liaising between discontented Arab sheikhs and a British Government that encouraged them. Extrovertly donning white Arab robes, the daredevil Lawrence was wounded several times, captured and tortured by the Turks. All these adventures made him natural star material. But there is little evidence that his contributions were any more significant than any other key members of the Arab Bureau in Cairo. Lawrence was essentially a creation of the British Government, which manipulated and massaged his fame; consequently he became one of the first manufactured celebrities in history. Like David Livingstone, Lawrence had a journalist working for an American newspaper on hand as a willing hagiographer: in London in 1919, the war correspondent Lowell

FAME BECOMES A PROBLEM

Thomas began a hugely successful series of illustrated lectures titled 'With Allenby in Palestine and Lawrence in Arabia'. The second segment was the one the public talked about, and Thomas's show became a big hit, even featuring on the Royal Command Performance. It also helped that Arab exoticism was in vogue at the time; two years later Rudolph Valentino was confirmed as a worldwide celebrity, playing a desert chieftain in *The Sheik*.

Whatever the reasons, the British adopted Lawrence as an authentic hero. Yet he was one of the first celebrities to feel unsettled by this new brand of fame. Those who advanced his cause as a celebrity mainly required that he be handsome, brave, charming and dashing, the very image of a cinema matinee idol. In truth, he was a complex figure. Certainly he had ambitions for Arabia, and the right chiselled features for fame at home. But he was small, shy, neurotic, homosexual and tortured by self-loathing – hardly the qualities his boosters were looking for.

He also had a decidedly ambiguous attitude towards his own celebrity. His friend George Bernard Shaw phrased it brilliantly, describing Lawrence 'backing bashfully into the limelight'. Part of Lawrence thrived on fame, but a bigger part of him despised it. After his Arabian exploits he did whatever he could to lower his public profile. At an audience with King George V in 1918, he refused to accept the DSO. In 1922 he enlisted in the ranks of the Royal Air Force under an assumed name. When the *Daily Express* gleefully exposed his secret new identity, he went undercover again, joining the Royal Tank Corps under yet another name, later re-enlisting in the RAF. And when he died in a motorcycle accident in 1935 in the small English village where he lived, significantly few neighbours knew of his real identity.

Lawrence was among the first to discover that negotiating modern fame involved a degree of play-acting. There was a pressure to assume a public identity, even one that might be contrary to one's private self.

Charles Lindbergh became another. Like Lawrence, he had a face that would not look out of place in close-up on a cinema screen. In 1927 he was literally an overnight sensation when he became the first man to fly non-stop across the Atlantic, from New York to Paris, in his plane the Spirit of St Louis. The feat made him a worldwide folk hero, and four million people lined the streets of New York for his homecoming tickertape parade. Lindbergh would have been happy if his adoring public (and a press that fed them news of his fame) had disappeared from his life at this precise moment. But they didn't.

In fairness, Lindbergh had been shrewd enough to project how momentous an occasion his transatlantic flight might be. He had managed to convince a consortium of businessmen to underwrite the flight – which incidentally carried the handsome sum of $25,000 in prize money. And even before his plane lifted off from New York, he had assured his future wealth by doing something celebrities had begun to do in the previous decade, sponsoring commercial products. He already had deals with Mobil Oil, Wright Aeronautical, AC spark plugs and Vacuum Oil in his pocket.

His huge miscalculation was to imagine he could complete his amazing flight, bask briefly in universal applause, then quietly dictate the terms of his own fame for the rest of his life. The media didn't work that way. They saw the tickertape parade as merely a first chapter of what might be a long-running narrative about various aspects of Lindbergh's private life. So the two sides entrenched themselves. The press wanted to know more about 'Lindy'. He stayed resolutely silent, and his reluctance to indulge in his new celebrity came across as haughtiness. Still the press pursued him. Lindbergh made a good marriage, to Anne Morrow, daughter of the US ambassador to Mexico, and the couple spent many hours flying together, in part to escape the barrage of media interest. On one occasion, they even made a temporary escape to Japan, only to find eager pressmen waiting for them.

This discomfiture turned to tragedy in 1932 when their two-year-old baby, Charles Jr., was kidnapped, held to ransom and murdered. It was the crime story of the decade, and the media followed it relentlessly until 1936, when Bruno Richard Hauptmann was tried, found guilty and executed for the crime. In later years Anne Morrow Lindbergh would blame the relentless publicity surrounding her family for her son's kidnap and murder. But the press did not leave the couple alone even after Charles Jr.'s death. When their second son Jon was born in 1935, journalists sideswiped their car, wrenching open a door in order to photograph the baby. Appalled, the Lindberghs decided to leave America for a spell, and moved to London.

Only twenty-five years before this happened, the fame industry was in such an embryonic state that America's film stars were not even credited by their own names. The fame virus had taken hold shortly afterwards, and was now spreading uncontrollably, voraciously consuming celebrities, would-be celebrities and fans alike. For those who could ride its wave, it still seemed an attractive proposition. But in its wake, lives were being ruined, and sometimes prematurely ended, and its victims had begun to appreciate what a Faustian pact it represented. The process had taken just one generation.

3
Who Needs Fame?

RULE THREE:
Celebrity behaviour is rooted in a type of personality disorder

Do people choose fame, or does it choose them? If we accept the proposition that modern-day celebrity is no longer necessarily tied to extraordinary achievement, what does this tell us about people who, as Daniel Boorstin put it, become 'well known for their well-knownness'? One imagines they might be of a type; and in broad terms, they emphatically are.

Within the literature of psychology can be found a list of diagnostic criteria for individuals with histrionic personality disorder, which is defined as 'a pervasive pattern of excessive emotionality and attention-seeking', as indicated by at least four of the following eight characteristics.

1 Constantly seeks or demands reassurance, approval or praise.
2 Is inappropriately sexually seductive in appearance or behaviour.
3 Is overly concerned with physical attractiveness.
4 Expresses emotion with inappropriate exaggeration (e.g. embraces casual acquaintances with excessive ardour, uncontrollable sobbing on minor sentimental occasions, has temper tantrums).
5 Is uncomfortable in situations in which he or she is not the centre of attention.
6 Displays rapidly shifting and shallow expression of emotions.
7 Is self-centred, actions being directed towards obtaining immediate satisfaction; has no tolerance for the frustration of delayed gratification.
8 Has a style of speech that is excessively impressionistic and lacking in detail (e.g. when asked to describe mother, can be no more specific than 'she was a beautiful person').

These characteristics sound alarmingly familiar. One could easily apply many of them to the parade of celebrities who flit across our television screens in the role of quiz-show host, talk-show guest, programme presenter or actor. I would say the majority of famous people I have met exhibit easily four or more of the above attributes.

There should be no real surprise about this. The very word 'histrionic' derives from an old Latin word meaning 'actor'; and a disproportionate number of famous people today are, in their public persona, actors of one sort or another; what binds them together above all is their exhibitionism. Still, it is dispiriting to observe that modes of behaviour associated with the most celebrated among us are rooted in a type of personality disorder.

It would be easy to ascribe all these traits to the famous, and assume that they all shared them to varying degrees. This is not the case, though everyone who regularly meets celebrities in their professional lives has favourite 'war stories' about unattractive behaviour. An excess of fame, an excess of wealth and indeed an excess of excess can easily exacerbate personality traits that already seem dysfunctional. One of the most common behaviour traits among the famous is a petulant self-absorption of a kind that would seem grotesque in 'ordinary' people.

One story often heard in film industry circles concerns actress Demi Moore, who was shooting the film *GI Jane* in Florida when a contractual obligation required her to be in New York over a weekend to publicize *Striptease*, a film she had made earlier. The company producing *Striptease* offered a private jet for her to travel to New York. But this was not enough. She claimed she needed to arrive with her retinue, including her own make-up assistant and her hairdresser; *two* private jets were needed.

A stand-off ensued. The company told her the hugely expensive demand was excessive. Moore dug her heels in. For the role of GI Jane her hair was closely cropped, and to appear before the media to publicize *Striptease*, she needed to look more as she did in that film. A wig would be necessary and only her hairdresser could make it look right. There was no question, apparently, of any members of her party travelling on a scheduled flight. Eventually, she prevailed and a second private jet was provided. Moore arrived in New York, and flounced into her suite at the Manhattan hotel where the media were gathered.

Her assistants danced attendance on her; her make-up was applied and her wig teased and combed until it looked perfect. These preparations made her late for a scheduled press conference and she was anxiously, though politely, summoned. Finally Moore stepped into an elevator that would take her down to the waiting media. She gazed at her own image in its mirrored walls, said: 'Naaah, it looks all wrong,' tore the wig off her head, and strolled into the press conference as GI Jane, with her hair closely cropped.

As an example of self-centred behaviour, it would be hard to emulate. But in my experience the actor Richard Dreyfuss does his best. The last time we met, we had lunch in an Italian restaurant in London, where he discussed a TV movie he had made portraying the gangster Meyer Lansky. At the end of the meal, he thrust the bill at me with the enchanting comment, 'I'll let you pay. After all, I'm sure the pleasure has been mostly yours.'

Dreyfuss was mistaken, as it happens. I had met him previously, and had always been struck by his arrogance. On one occasion, he told me a story about being a young man of thirty. At that time he had already starred in *Jaws* and *Close Encounters of the Third Kind*, two of the most successful films ever made, and he was the youngest man ever to win a Best Actor Oscar. 'I was in this hotel room in New York,' he said. 'I'm fifty-eight storeys above Central Park. There's champagne, a little cocaine, a beautiful girl, a big picture window. Suddenly the girl turns to me and says: "Do you think you deserve all this?" I looked around. And I said: "Yeah. I *do*."' He laughed sardonically, and explained that this was before his fast living caught up with him. Addicted to alcohol and drugs, one night he wrapped his Mercedes convertible around a palm tree on a canyon above Beverly Hills. He survived, but was arrested for possessing cocaine and Percodan; a court ordered him into rehab. And that was the beginning of what Dreyfuss terms his 'resurrection'. An intriguing choice of word, but consistent with a man who uses the royal we or refers to himself in the third person, as Richard.

Some of this is routine vanity, though Dreyfuss goes further. In the past he has employed a political consultant, who monitors and keeps him abreast of developments in the Middle East, and advises him where his sympathies might lie. This is a level of self-importance beyond parody, summoning an image of Israeli soldiers preparing to bombard a Palestinian encampment with mortar fire. One says to another: 'Look, before we do this, let's stop and think: how will it play with Richard Dreyfuss?'

Fame, of course, bestows the opportunity to shore up one's weaknesses in public to an astonishing extent. In 1999 I went to Thailand to watch the shooting of *The Beach*, starring Leonardo di Caprio. Set largely on an idyllic beach on an offshore island, it had become controversial locally; Thai environmental groups had protested the island's ecology was being ruined by the film crew uprooting plant life and bulldozing sand dunes to make the location conform to a cinematic ideal of an island paradise. When I talked to di Caprio and asked him about these protests, it was clear he had absolutely no notion of the complexity of the arguments. Quite simply, he was out of his depth. He insisted on the film's producer sitting with him throughout the interview, and he anxiously relied on him to help him out with his answers.

'It's one of those situations where it gets into politics,' he said, dully. He turned to the producer. 'Can I say politics?'

'Yes,' said the producer, patiently.

Criticism of his lack of grasp about these issues clearly stung di Caprio, who was at the time, in the wake of *Titanic*, the world's hottest young actor. Even so, his strategy for dealing with the Thai criticism was shameless, even by the standards of the industry in which he works. Effectively he promoted himself as the young celebrity spokesman for all matters environmental, letting it be known that he cared deeply about the future of the planet. And how successful was this strategy? Within eighteen months of his stumbling performance in Thailand, di Caprio was on American network television, interviewing President Clinton, no less, about such matters as greenhouse gases and global warming. One had to admit it, his nerve was breathtaking.

A desire to be constantly at the centre of attention is a common by-product of fame. It seems especially noticeable among female celebrities. In the past, one observed it in Joan Collins, Cher, Elizabeth Taylor and Marilyn Monroe; at various times in their respective lives, it seemed that their every action was designed to create headlines, and one grew tired of reading or hearing about them. (The media find it easier to write vacuous nonsense about famous women – their appearance, their fluctuating weight, their dress sense are considered legitimate subject matter.) At the time of writing, in 2002, the figures fitting this description of media overkill would include various Spice Girls present and past, Britney Spears, Jennifer Lopez and, inevitably, Madonna, whose entire career to date has involved her own negotiations with fame and her careful manipulation of her image.

On occasion Madonna may concede, as she once did to me, that she is tired of celebrity and wants no more of it. It is a surprising request, coming from one who has long craved publicity so abjectly; the surprise is that she feels she has a private self to protect. She has flourished in the spotlight for so many years that one speculates about what kind of life she might have without cameras pointed in her direction. In the 1991 documentary, *Truth or Dare*, also tellingly known as *In Bed With Madonna*, her then boyfriend Warren Beatty grumbles about her reluctance to live life outside a frame: 'She doesn't even want to live off-camera, much less talk.'

The American critic Neal Gabler has written of *Truth or Dare*: 'She made her life movie about her life movie', and observed that in the film Madonna takes 'what might be called a post-modernist view of celebrity'. What I think he means is her willingness to let her audience in on the 'secret' that she is pulling off a kind of con trick. Throughout the film, she downplays her talents, admitting she is not the best singer, dancer or actress. At one point, addressing the camera directly, she asks: 'Who do I think I am, trying to pull this off?' Gabler has the answer: 'She was a conceptual performance artist whose truest art was the art of promoting Madonna.'

There is something in this. Madonna's stance towards her audience brings to mind the song 'Razzle Dazzle' by Fred Ebb and John Kander from their musical *Chicago*, with its refrain: 'Razzle dazzle 'em, and they'll make you a star!'

The song, of course, is about the entertainer as con artist. Daniel Boorstin once observed of the legendary American showman P. T. Barnum that he was successful not because he knew people could be fooled, but because he knew people enjoyed being fooled, especially if you showed them how it was being done.

Similarly, Madonna makes her audience complicit in such a con trick: 'Who do I think I am?' Yet ultimately it is a trick and nothing more. What Gabler does not add is that she poses a question about herself that did not need asking, and then answers it at length. This may be post-modernism, but it is also a means to ensure the audience's attention stays on her; it is a form of self-absorption far beyond levels most of us could imagine.

Yet there is another side to her career that suggests vulnerability, even pathos. Madonna, in common with a small number of contemporary artists (David Bowie comes to mind), has chosen to re-invent her persona over the years. This can be read as a canny device to stay one step ahead of one's audience, and a means to prevent them from tiring of a persona that remains stable. But what does it say about such an artist's sense of identity? It can also be read as a form of pandering, a willingness to jettison one's real character traits and adopt new, artificially introduced ones – all for fear of public rejection. One recalls a phrase frequently used by the humanistic psychologist Erich Fromm: 'I am as you desire me.' Viewed in this light, the celebrity strategy of re-invention seems piteous.

Bowie, at least, has synchronized his re-inventions with his artistic output. In a period spanning some fifteen years, he adopted and discarded identities with alarming speed. He emerged in the late 1960s as a spiky-haired, snappily-dressed London mod, but then came the costume changes. In 1970 he posed for an album cover in drag; successively he allowed himself to be perceived as a foppish, long-haired young aesthete, the cosmetically enhanced glam-rock superstar Ziggy Stardust, and the futuristic Aladdin Sane. Next, Bowie opted for the sharp, tailored lines and the faintly fascist persona of the 'thin white duke', before unveiling his next, more relaxed preppy wardrobe for his *Young Americans* album. On the cover of *Low*, he resembled an earnest, itinerant young student in a duffle coat; on *Heroes*, one could mistake him for an outspoken leather-clad intellectual, debating an obscure point in some European coffee house. It now seems almost prophetic that one of Bowie's early hits was titled 'Changes'.

In his heyday, he actually took great pains to confuse people about his identity. During his period as the faintly monstrous Ziggy Stardust, he hired as his office staff a group of people from Andy Warhol's

Factory who had also appeared in Warhol's play *Pork*. 'I thought the cast looked great, so I hired them,' Bowie told me. 'So all these nutcases, these crazed New York people were working for me. I thought, whoo-hoo, we'll have some fun with this lot!' He designated as his publicist a young magenta-haired groupie known as Cherry Vanilla: 'I'd say, "Cherry, go off and do my interview for me." She'd say, "But I don't know anything about you." I'd tell her, "Say what you think I'd say." So she went out and made up answers to all these questions about me, so the whole fabric of that period is totally incorrect. I can't follow half of it myself. Everyone would say what they thought I'd say, or maybe what they wanted me to. I was intrigued with the whole idea of setting images against each other. So I used to have people going out and changing the truth for me.'

Bowie viewed these ventures that calculatedly blurred his identity rather like conceptual art events; they also enhanced the intrigue and mystique surrounding his Ziggy Stardust persona. Madonna's re-inventions, less focused and specific and lacking much of an agenda, hint at personal conflicts in a way Bowie's do not. In her time, she has adopted the stage persona of a cowgirl, clad in gingham skirts. She has presented herself as a movie star from the Golden Age of the 1940s, as a dominatrix, and as a futuristic icon with pointed cones covering her breasts. On video she has portrayed herself as sexually voracious, clutching a crucifix with an expression hinting at both guilt and lust. More recently, since her marriage to British film director Guy Ritchie, she has been pictured in London (off-stage but still within a frame) as a down-to-earth mother and wife, performing humdrum domestic duties such as washing a family car. At times, she resembles a small girl let loose in her mother's old clothes closet, trying on costumes at random, then throwing them off because they fail to make her feel sufficiently pretty or content.

Madonna and Bowie are two very different artists who have one thing in common: they have managed to harness their complex feelings about fame and identity and to exploit them in the service of their careers. They have managed to integrate the exhibitionist strands of their personality into their performance and their relationship with their audience.

What may appear more surprising is the willingness of other celebrities to bare their souls by admitting to personality disorders, dysfunction, addiction and various kinds of victimhood that may have scarred them. The actor Michael Douglas has confessed to being a 'sex addict'; Robert Downey Jr.'s travails with drugs are better known than his acting career. The comedienne Roseanne Barr admits to being abused as a child; scarcely a week goes by without some famous person announcing they are undergoing rehabilitation for problems relating to the abuse of alcohol, painkillers or other substances.

These weaknesses and dysfunctions belong purely in the personal realm, and bear no relation to the gifts that made these people in the first place (except, occasionally, their temporary inability to do their job). Yet the confession of these problems is paraded proudly, as if the problems are desirable add-ons to the celebrities' public personae; they turn into what marketing executives call a USP, or unique selling point. Most of us, confronted with such problems in our lives, would decide to deal with them privately and discreetly. So why, in celebrity circles, do personality disorders or haunting secrets become commodities to advertise to the world? A few reasons seem plausible. One is that the very identity of celebrities, especially those without notable talents to fall back upon, is validated by their constant appearances in public. It follows, then, that they can best process their personal tragedies or problems in a public context. If these people feel they have no meaningful existence outside the frame, then their personal problems have no meaning either, unless they are being witnessed and analysed by a viewing public.

Another reason is that the admission of such 'weaknesses' helps to humanize celebrities, soften their image and give their audience a feeling of empathy with them. Because such admissions are usually made on the celebrity's own terms (that is to say, mediated and curtailed by their press representatives) this empathy can be achieved without a celebrity actually having to spend extra personal time with that audience. If famous people choose to elaborate on the facts behind their misfortune, it often happens on TV talk shows, where questioning is soft and respectful.

Closely related is another reason. It has to do with guilt. The disclosure of problems in celebrities' private lives is often expressed in terms that resemble a form of atonement, but atonement for what?

Their fame, of course, their wealth, and all the attention they can muster without ever feeling they quite deserve it. There is a subtext to such disclosures: 'You may think my life is perfect and enviable, but here is proof that any jealousy you may harbour towards me is unjustified.' Later I shall examine the curious dichotomy of fan worship, involving adoration on the one hand and hostility on the other. Confessions by celebrities that their lives are less than perfect can be used to allay that hostility.

This may sound chillingly calculating, but then celebrities' spin doctors are paid to make precisely such calculations. An admission of some secret problem or conflict can, if handled adroitly, even strengthen the bond between celebrity and fan; it makes fans feel vested in the celebrities' well-being, and if they have confessed to some weakness, wrong-doing or 'inappropriate' behaviour, it is within the fans' province to forgive them. This goes some way to evening up the imbalance in the relationship, and allows fans to think of their relationship with a celebrity like some long-term friendship, one with ups and downs that must be weathered.

So it is that famous people will own up to problems with booze and drugs, sex addiction, even a propensity for violence (for which they receive anger counselling). All these tendencies can help to flesh them out in the public mind, to make them seem more human, more like the rest of us, while doing nothing to jeopardize the 'brand' of their careers. The one notable exception, shamefully, is the admission of homosexuality; if we were to take today's population of famous people at their word, they would represent the most determinedly heterosexual population in the Western world. Celebrities will more readily confess the most egregious examples of anti-social, swinish behaviour than come out of the closet and declare themselves gay. Predictably, this reluctance is rooted in an economic nostrum. The theory is often voiced throughout the entertainment industry, itself heavily populated by behind-the-scenes gay people, that performers who declare their homosexuality inevitably lose their popular appeal; the leading man known to be gay can no longer convincingly play a character wooing a woman on screen. (He can, of course: it's an ability known as acting. But still the creepy superstition prevails.)

Still, the sight of celebrities 'confessing' their various Achilles' heels can be an unsettling sight. The actress Melanie Griffith has her own website, in which she appears in a long white flowing dress and invites fans in her distinctive Betty Boop voice to join her in Avalon, a fictional land where there is 'pure beauty, serenity, tranquillity and peace'. Pictures of Avalon on the web page show a place with still lakes, ancient pillars, blossoms, antique wrought-iron doors and blossom sprinkled everywhere. It was on this website that Griffith recorded her selectively factual 'recovery diary' after being admitted to a Los Angeles hospital for her addiction to the painkiller Vicodin late in 2000 – merely the latest episode in her long history of drugs and alcohol abuse. This soul-baring has an economic basis, however: Griffith also uses the site to advertise jewellery from her own Goddess range, and plug various business enterprises (and, to be fair, charities) involving friends. Visiting her site is a queasy experience.

There is another compelling reason why celebrities find it easy to trumpet their personality disorders, dysfunctions, addictions and various other problems so loudly: in their world, they are not so far removed from the norm. In his 1995 book *Starstruck*, American communications professor Jib Fowles examined a hundred celebrities from the last century whose careers had been completed. He defined the traits of stars, studied their origins, how they rose within their chosen fields, and the arc of their professional lives. His survey showed that stars have shorter lives than most people, with higher death rates from cirrhosis (a disease closely linked to alcohol), murder, kidney disease, ulcers, accidents and suicide. The group surveyed by Fowles suffered self-inflicted deaths at a rate three times above the average. What does all this prove? In terms of cause and effect, it is hard to be conclusive. It may be that the effects of fame destabilize people, or it may be that unstable or erratic people are more likely to be famous in the first place, due to obsessive drives or their increased tendency to risk-taking. It brings us full circle to the question: what kinds of individuals become famous? Do certain people choose fame, or does it choose them?

It is no surprise that people choose fame. To the outsider it appears to be a condition of extraordinary allure. But we may cautiously conclude that people who embrace it and single-mindedly pursue it are those prepared to reject almost every vestige of the lives they led in obscurity. Overnight fame, in particular, can wreak havoc on a personality because of the outside factors it often brings in its wake. These include the break-up of marriages or long-term relationships; an enormous change in one's financial state; a move from a familiar environment; a new residence; being surrounded by a completely new set of people, both personally and professionally. Any one of these factors is jolting enough, but taken together they can induce stress and discontent to an alarming degree.

Even David Bowie, who, as has been discussed, seemed to manage the changes in his life and career coolly and with a good deal of shrewdness, fell victim to fame's more rancid side-effects. Late in 1975, he was twenty-eight years old, living in a huge house on Doheny Drive in Los Angeles, at the height of his fame – and addicted to drugs. 'That was the lowest point of my life, when I thought drugs had taken my life away from me. I felt as though I would probably die in the next year or so, and it was probably all over. I'd lost all contact with the real world. I was no longer socially interactive. When they say a man feels like somebody's grabbed his soul and plucked it out of him, it really felt like that. I was zombie-like, as though my soul had been taken away from me. It was more than depressing, it was like being thrown into an abyss. Everything was done for me. There were months when I never left the house.'

Bowie also believes his fame, and the easy availability of addictive drugs, attracted the wrong kind of acquaintances. 'You find yourself with an entourage, none of whom you know very well, but all of whom seem firmly of the opinion that you need them more than anyone else in your life. You wake up mornings and find people in your house you just don't recognize. And apparently they've been there the night before as well. There was money coming in, so the other people around me at the time were perfectly content for me to remain in that condition. It was just this strange, ephemeral world of the wrong people and the wrong inclinations.'

Around this time Bowie co-wrote the song 'Fame' with John Lennon, one of the most famous victims of his own celebrity. As the song puts it, fame 'makes a man take things over', 'lets him loose, hard to swallow', and 'puts you there where things are hollow'.

Bowie made a conscious attempt to wrench himself out of this life.

In 1976 he left America and moved to Berlin. 'I tried to come back to street level again. Proper streets, not the fashion streets or drug streets of LA, but supermarket streets. I went back to driving a car, buying cigarettes myself. Really silly, common things for everyone else, but for me, a big deal.' He found a new equilibrium. 'I was walking around, virtually anonymous. People in Berlin are so blasé and cynical about the effects and the reasons for fame and celebrity that it really doesn't matter who you are. It was wonderful to be able to do that.'

If Bowie's attitude towards celebrity is as jaundiced an account as one may hear, it does not detract from his original desire to be famous. 'I had this burning, overriding feeling that [success] would happen,' he told me. 'I must say that I actually didn't have any doubt about it. Ever since I was eight years old, when I was given my first Little Richard record, I said: "I want to do that, I want to be just like that." It never occurred to me that I could do other than succeed at some point . . . it took a lot to thwart me. I didn't really see any obstacle as something that couldn't be overcome somehow or other. I was the "sensitive artist", but I could endure a lot.'

He consciously chose fame, and even had some sense of its drawbacks before he attained it. By that time, there was substantial evidence, stretching back half a century, that fame was not all it was cracked up to be. Clark Gable famously voiced his doubts about the fame virus to David Niven on the occasion of the mysterious death of Hollywood actress Thelma Todd in 1935; she had been found in her parked car, and was found to have died from carbon monoxide poisoning.

Gable told Niven: 'We all have a contract with the public. In us they see themselves or what they would like to be . . . they love to put us on a pedestal and worship us . . . but *they've* read the small print and most of us haven't. So when we get knocked off by gangsters, like Thelma did, or hooked on booze or dope or . . . just get sold, the public feels satisfied. Yeah, it's a good idea to read that small print.'

Yet Gable's own career suggests a man with huge ambition. He saw his first play when he was fourteen years old and was so star-struck he began working as a stagehand for no money. His father moved him to Oklahoma to work at drilling for oil; but he was so smitten with theatre that at twenty-one he left his father to join a troupe of travelling players led by Josephine Dillon, an experienced actress fourteen years

Gable's senior. She took an interest in him and coached him as an actor; eventually they married and moved to Hollywood. Dillon helped him obtain some work as a film extra, but then could advance his career no further. He promptly dumped her and struck out on his own; a year after their divorce in 1930 he became a top MGM leading man.

Gable's story is by no means extraordinary; in fact it has classic elements. Note his absolute certainty about what he wanted to do from early adolescence, his willingness to leave his father, and his rejection of his first wife once she had given him an entrée into the film world. In his later years, Gable developed into an accomplished actor, but then, screen acting is hardly the most rigorous discipline; looking good and breaking into the business in the first place are the most important factors. Gable, who looked good, had the drive and ambition to get a foot in the door.

In terms of fame, though, drive and ambition are merely entry qualifications. A study by a team from the University of Minnesota in 2000 surveyed all forty-one American presidents for common personality traits. As a group, they were found to be manipulative, bullying, disorganized and devious. They were emphatically not straightforward, vulnerable, paralysed by outbreaks of conscience or invariably wedded to telling the truth. They tended to conform to our stereotype of figures born to lead: stubborn, assertive and socially disagreeable.

This is unsurprising: who expects famous people to adhere to personality norms? Most of us are dimly aware that the route to fame is built on single-mindedness and ambition, no matter how placid, pleasant or 'ordinary' celebrities may strive to make themselves appear.

None of this should necessarily inspire pity for the famous. With each year that passes, we find the celebrity community increasingly populated not by those who are talented or meritorious, but those who inhabit it primarily because they want to. Yet, as ordinary people ironically ask when they watch the famous parading their celebrity or wealth, are they happy? The evidence suggests large numbers of them are not, that fame serves as a glittering mask for a host of problems, including disillusionment with fame's nature, and its inadequacy at bringing fulfilment.

Given, then, that famous people already exhibit traits that one might deem disorders when they start out on the road to celebrity, is it any surprise that the condition of fame – the isolation, the sudden separation from one's familiar surroundings, the possibility of spending money and exercising power as never before – only exacerbates those disorders? One could go further and assert that life within the frame is an unhealthy place to be, an environment that can seriously damage a personality that may already be bruised. It is really no wonder that many celebrities give the impression of instability. But as we shall see, compared to some of their fans, they are paragons of mental health.

4

The Fans

RULE FOUR:
Fans love you – right up to the point they loathe and despise you

Off-screen, the comic actor Steve Martin is not the most ingratiating of actors, and coaxing him into amiable conversation was like pulling teeth, even when it involved something so self-serving as talking up his latest movie. A lunch I had with him in Los Angeles might have been perfectly unmemorable but for one incident. During the main course, a large, pudgy, ill-dressed man lurched towards our table and thrust a dog-eared autograph book at him.

'Steve,' he said, in a voice that brooked no interruption, 'I love your work! I'm one of your biggest fans, I've seen all your movies and your stand-up shows, and I wondered if you'd sign . . .'

Martin's eyes narrowed, and he held up one hand to stem the barrage of words. He pointed out he was having lunch, he was in the middle of a conversation and anyway he didn't really like signing autographs. The man's face immediately clouded over. He snapped his grubby book shut, turned on his heel and walked off.

'Well, screw you!' he said over his shoulder. He addressed his next comment to a couple sitting a few tables away. 'A big shot!' he said scornfully, jerking his head towards Martin.

Celebrities will recognize in this exchange a perfect paradigm of their relationship with fans. It's a binary thing. They love you – right up to the point they loathe and despise you. It's a common symptom of the fame virus as fans experience it.

Nan Beecher-Moore, a London-based therapist whose clients include famous people from various walks of life, argues that the dichotomy between adoration and hostility is a fundamental component of fan worship. 'Oh, sure, because the famous person doesn't live up to expectations. There's a fury, because they don't live up to who we want or expect them to be. Which is why fame is so dangerous.'

Of course, whatever strong feelings fans have for celebrities are based on false presumptions of intimacy. We have seen how the cinematic close-up first revealed film stars to ordinary people in the most minute detail and how, when you gaze upon an attractive face on a huge movie screen, an intimate relationship is forged. But it is a one-way relationship. A fan may make a heavy emotional investment in tracking the life and career of, say, Michelle Pfeiffer, and if he is at the delusional end of the fandom spectrum he may have convinced himself that he and Pfeiffer have some kind of relationship that bonds them together; it is only he who understands her and sympathizes with the fluctuations in her life.

Let us pause to observe that nothing in the way star actors are presented in public does much to tarnish this delusion. On screen, the Michelle Pfeiffers of the world are quite literally presented in their most attractive, alluring light. And when we see them on television as themselves, on talk-shows, or doing interviews to promote their work, they are usually polite, smiling and full of good grace, all the better to lure people to the product; that is, their latest movie.

Even average fans can take this as evidence of an invitation to intimacy. (Surprise at the disjunction between public persona and reality is not confined to fans. I once spent two hours interviewing Michelle Pfeiffer alone in her Hollywood production offices, and she turned out to be a cooler, even chillier character than I expected.) But fans' attempts at intimacy are doomed. They approach stars armed with copious foreknowledge about them; the stars for their part know nothing about the fan who looms towards them, beaming with pleasure while proffering an autograph book – certainly not enough to guarantee that he or she isn't crazy or violent.

Thus the presumed intimacy is nipped in the bud at its first instance of open expression, by a star rebuffing advances which in fairness would seem inappropriate and excessive in any other context. And what worsens the situation is that the fan often feels some sense of entitlement in regard to the star. He has stayed devoted to her through her good times and her crises; he may even have sat through her less well-regarded movies with no complaint. Surely this loyalty merits some warmth, or at least politeness, at the very moment the fan has summoned up the courage to beg for some token of recognition, even in the trivial form of a kind word, a minute or two spent in conversation, or an autograph. If a rebuff comes, the fan can feel like a lover spurned; his sense of hurt can easily turn to anger – and in extreme cases, thoughts of revenge.

Of course, it doesn't even need a rebuff for tragedy to occur. There is a famous photograph of John Lennon signing a copy of his album *Double Fantasy* for a young fan named Mark David Chapman. It was taken just hours before Chapman showed up outside the Dakota Building in New York, where Lennon lived, and shot him dead.

I have watched interactions between fans and stars over the years, and it seems to me that from both sides they are a necessary evil. Fans latch on to their favourite celebrities for whatever psychological needs they meet, and in the vast majority of cases it's a harmless pastime and source of pleasure. Yet their adoration can easily turn to contempt if frustrated or rebuffed.

For their part, famous people understand that fans represent their economic base. They perceive the need to keep fans content (and constantly consuming their products) but try to keep them at arm's length whenever possible; they prefer fans never to intrude on their everyday activities. One can understand this. Cast an eye over groups of people who go out of their way to meet a celebrity, by waiting for an hour at a stage door, for example. They rarely strike you as types with whom you would willingly spend much time. There may be individual exceptions to this rule in every such crowd, but en masse, there is something a little deranged and wild-eyed about them; they give off a faint whiff of psychosis. Watching fans approach a celebrity for a photo, an autograph or conversation, I have been struck by the lack of social skills they exhibit, through maybe either a notable gracelessness or an alarming, swiftly discernible neediness. Invariably, their behaviour is founded in an inflated and unjustified sense of familiarity. However one defines it, it is no prize to be the recipient of such uninvited individual attentions.

Oddly, it's the excessively devoted who most often trigger feelings of contempt from celebrities. Fans who can rattle off how many times they have seen an actor's films, or attended a singer's concerts, these are the ones who make their heroes feel embarrassed and uneasy. Many celebrities have their own entourages, which become a breeding ground for an atmosphere of contempt towards fans. A tight little circle of 'us against them' is established, and outsiders and fans ('civilians', as I have heard them dismissively called) become regarded with increasing disdain. This contempt is by no means a recent phenomenon; there are long-standing examples of movie stars voicing their discomfort about their followers. Tyrone Power called crowds of fans 'the monster'. Tony Curtis noted: 'It's like having Alzheimer's disease. You don't know anybody, but they all know you.' Esther Williams summarized a few rules for dealing with fans: 'Walk fast. Don't stop and shake hands. You touch them, they don't touch you.' (Presumably, staying immersed in water also helped her.)

For the most part, being a fan is a blameless pastime that stems from understandable desires: sometimes, the fantasized relationship with the stars meets a need for companionship and familiarity that may be missing in real life. Yet there can also be a sense of affiliation with other fans in this pursuit; there was no question that fans of pop idols in their early careers – Frank Sinatra, Elvis Presley, the Beatles, the Rolling Stones – bonded with each other, even if it was a generational bonding that asserted their musical preferences over those of their parents.

Most of us would make indulgent assumptions about adult fans who go a stage further, plastering the walls of their house with pictures of their heroes, and filling rooms with memorabilia. We might note that such rooms become informal 'shrines', highlighting the semi-religious fervour of fan worship, and how many stars are now referred to as 'pop icons', say, or 'movie gods'. We may assume these people are introverted, that they lack a strong sense of their own identity, that their fan worship must be rooted in a rich, active fantasy life. We may even speculate that in emotional terms they seem never to have outgrown adolescence. Most of us would feel inclined to leave them in peace to pursue their innocent interest, yet it is a rare celebrity who would not feel uncomfortable at being confronted by such evidence of fan worship.

Celebrities generally feel relaxed when fans restrict their devotional acts to the passive consumption of the products they are offering: the buying of records or tickets for concerts or movies. Only when fans begin to demand payback from stars for their financial and emotional outlay does conflict arise.

In rare instances, a star's fans become incorporated in the public image he is projecting. This happened in the case of Tom Jones, and it began accidentally. In 1968 Jones was singing at the Copacabana nightclub in New York and was sweating so profusely that a female fan walked from the audience and offered him what he assumed was a napkin to wipe his brow. The napkin turned out to be her panties. After syndicated columnist Earl Wilson reported this incident, it quickly became a ritual of Jones's stage shows that women would hurl their underwear on stage for him. In Las Vegas, hotel room keys supplemented their panties. His then manager Gordon Mills seized upon this phenomenon as a publicity gimmick to heighten Jones's fame and capitalize on his smouldering sexuality.

In 1990 I co-wrote a biography of Tom Jones, part of which detailed the tempestuous relationship between his management company and his fans, especially the members of the seventy-five Tom Jones fan clubs in America. All, it seems, proceeded smoothly in the early stages of his career; the underwear-tossing was viewed as a spontaneous bonus for Jones's image. But later, things turned sour. Those predominantly female fans who had followed his career since its beginnings in the mid-1960s no longer looked as young and nubile. Jones's management became concerned that his image could be besmirched by the overwhelming number of frumpy middle-aged housewives in the front rows of his stage shows. So they instigated a policy in such venues as Las Vegas: they would hold back seats for the first few rows of his shows, stroll through the town's casinos and give away free tickets for those seats to younger, attractive women who represented the demographic they wanted to attract. Of course, Jones's most ardent, long-standing fans were the very ones denied proximity to their idol by this policy, and fury in the fan clubs was widespread and profound.

Relations worsened further after Mills died and Jones's son Mark took over as his manager. He appointed his wife Donna as Jones's publicist, and she began dictating rules to fan club members, insisting they no longer call him Tom, but 'Mr Jones'. His management company sent his fan clubs an infamous letter, stating they could no longer automatically expect to visit him backstage after concerts. 'If your motivation for being a club is based on a personal moment with the artist, then your motivation is wrong.' The letter even detailed the gifts Jones preferred from fans: fruit, home-made food items, towels and champagne.

The letter was perceived as galling. While researching the biography, I spoke to a dozen US fan club organizers who were infuriated by its dismissive, presumptuous tone, and were convinced Jones had decided to dump his older fans. Their sense of hurt, anger and rejection was palpable. I spoke to a woman who identified herself only as Adele, who had jointly run his New Orleans fan club for eighteen years. 'What's so sad,' she said, 'what's so degrading, is that we'll probably keep doing this. I don't know why – we wouldn't take this kind of treatment from our husbands.'

At least Adele had the insight to realize she was getting the worst of a bad bargain. The horrors of what can happen when fan worship is taken to its logical conclusion were brilliantly described as long ago as 1939 in Nathanael West's classic novel *The Day of the Locust*, which ends in an appalling riot at a movie premiere, where frenzied fans lose control. West's thesis was that Hollywood is a place of false promises, a grotesque, corrupt dream factory that distorts the lives and aspirations of those who come under its spell. Tellingly, the character who most closely stands for Hollywood is a ruthlessly ambitious, whorish bit-part actress.

Many celebrities now have their own security handlers, who constantly accompany them in public and advise them on how to conduct themselves if they are to avoid being harassed by fans. Esther Williams's guidelines have come to be a model for celebrity behaviour towards fans. Avoidance of eye contact is a good policy; staying on the move in crowded streets is another. Autographs should only be signed when there seems no alternative, if possible without making conversation with the person requesting them, and preferably while talking about another matter entirely to a member of one's entourage. 'Never let the crazies think they own a part of you,' as a Hollywood security expert once expressed it to me.

Fans have their uses, of course. The managers of some celebrities have been known to pick out devoted but capable fans, and put their loyalty to positive use. In the past this often meant they could organize fan clubs, which typically involved scheduling regular meetings for fans. The star might even attend some of these meetings; it provided a means for devotion to be temporarily satisfied with an in-the-flesh meeting and a few moments of conversation with the adored one. Of course, putting a devoted fan in charge of such activity (which is tedious work) meant that the star's management company could offload it from its own employees; dealing with fans is notoriously time-consuming.

More recently, fans have set up official Internet sites (significantly, some are called 'shrines') devoted to the star. In this capacity, they often do something else the management company would rather not do: they become the celebrity's semi-official archivist. But generally, such channelling of fan worship is a useful way of mediating between a star and fans, and helping defuse the relationship.

Woody Allen, who famously caricatured fans as grotesques out of a Fellini movie in his 1980 film *Stardust Memories*, seems genuinely puzzled by their fulsome adoration. There is a telling scene in Barbara Kopple's documentary *Wild Man Blues* which follows Allen on tour in Europe with the New Orleans-style jazz band for which he plays clarinet. It shows Allen and his new wife Soon-Yi on a gondola in Venice, where they are hailed excitedly by a boatload of passing American tourists. Under his breath and from behind gritted teeth, he berates them: 'Yeah, yeah, they want my autograph,' he grouses. 'But they won't go and see my movies.'

Allen expounded on this theme when I talked to him in 2000. 'That scene is true, and it is sad,' he said. 'You would think in the United States that my films would do very well based on the amount of photographs that are taken of me and autographs I'm asked for. You'd think, my God!

'[Soon-Yi and I] once went on a weekend trip to Louisiana. From the moment we showed up, everyone was taking pictures, asking for autographs. You'd have thought when I walked through those streets and sat at the restaurants it was one of the Beatles. You'd have thought from the people around me I'd have to be the biggest star down there. But before that visit, when my pictures would open there, they'd drop dead at the box office. And it was the same after the visit. The attention given me while I was there was phenomenal. But those people definitely do not see my pictures.'

He misses the point, of course. From the viewpoint of fans (and of the media that feed them titbits of gossip about celebrities) the dependency of fame on achievement is no longer obligatory. Though Allen has continued to make films with clockwork regularity in a distinguished thirty-year career, he is equally famous for being famous. And in the last few years he has become especially famous for his relationship with Soon-Yi, which began in scandal; she is, after all, the adopted daughter of Mia Farrow, who was Allen's lover when the relationship began. Those fans who swarm around them care little for the ebb and flow of Allen's film oeuvre, they're just thrilled to encounter an infamous, high-profile, instantly recognizable and oddly contrasting celebrity couple.

Woody Allen is an artist who would prefer people to go and see all his movies, but never approach him directly. Steve Martin may well be another; one of his aides told me he dislikes shaking hands with people he has never met. But most celebrities I have met regard fans with at best a faint air of embarrassment and often something worse: a discernible mistrust.

Considering the worst-case scenarios, one can hardly blame them. After all, they know the stories. They know of John W. Hinckley Jr., who shot President Reagan because he wanted to impress actress Jodie Foster, the object of his desire. They know of Mark David Chapman, who assassinated John Lennon and said plaintively afterwards: 'I thought by killing him I would acquire his fame.' They know of the serial killer Andrew Cunanan, who worked his way up the ladder of infamy by despatching three increasingly wealthy, influential men before his final bloody coup, the murder of international designer Gianni Versace. And though it was over thirty years ago, they remember the murderous carnage wreaked by the members of Charles Manson's gang on the pregnant actress Sharon Tate and her glitzy Hollywood friends. Seven people died at the Manson Family's hands.

These are all well-known cases. Yet the mere fact of being truly famous is no prerequisite for being stalked, assaulted or killed. In 1989, I was living in the West Hollywood area of Los Angeles and was jogging one summer day around the streets of my neighbourhood when I came upon a crime scene. Police had sealed off the drive of an attractive small bungalow, but on its front doorstep one could easily see a pool of blood. It turned out to belong to Rebecca Shaeffer, a little-known twenty-two-year-old actress, who had been fatally shot by an obsessed nineteen-year-old fan. Robert John Bardo, from Tucson, Arizona, had stalked her for two years. He had written to her repeatedly and tried without success to meet her at the studios of Warner Bros., the producers of *My Sister Sam*, an innocent, long-forgotten TV sitcom in which she featured. Her death seemed especially jarring. Who on earth could feel so strongly about a pleasing but minor-league figure like Rebecca Shaeffer that he would kill her?

It seemed Bardo had seen Shaeffer playing a much more sexually provocative role in the film *Scenes from the Class Struggle in Beverly Hills*, and had become enraged. Soon afterwards, he wrote to a relative, 'I have an obsession with the unattainable. I have to eliminate what I cannot attain.' He hired a private detective, who for a $250 fee provided Bardo with Shaeffer's home address, which he obtained from California drivers' licence records. (US privacy laws would later be modified after this shameful disclosure.) Bardo persuaded his twenty-one-year-old brother to buy a .357 Magnum for him, travelled to Los Angeles, and put a bullet in Shaeffer's chest.

When such terrible things occur, two facts become clear. The first is that, as Americans invariably phrase it, in tones tinged with wistful regret, 'There's a lot of crazy people out there.' The second is that the presence in the world of so many stalkers, crazies and potential killers presents a quick-thinking entrepreneur with an ideal business opportunity. Cometh the hour, cometh the man, and in the wake of the Lennon and Reagan incidents, a certain Gavin de Becker was that man.

I first learned of Gavin de Becker in 1982, when I was given a bizarre assignment by *People* magazine. After Mark David Chapman and John Hinckley had committed their dreadful deeds, an intruder had been discovered in Cher's house, and the Hollywood community, a nervous, self-absorbed group at the best of times, had become openly paranoid. The acerbic comedienne Joan Rivers had taken the advice of a security expert, and was hosting self-defence awareness parties for women showbiz friends. I visited Rivers in her enormous Beverly Hills mansion, which had the most elaborate of security and alarm arrangements, and when I finally received clearance to drive in through its electric gates, three bodyguards were on the prowl. Rivers apparently failed to see any contradiction between hiring security experts to lecture her and her friends about their personal safety, and then contacting a national magazine to publicize that she had done so.

'We sit around and talk and practise,' she told me. 'You've heard of cheese and wine parties? Well, these are cheese, wine and Mace parties.' And indeed she and her friends were being tutored in how to spray a can of Mace to ward off unwelcome intruders or potential attackers.

Gavin de Becker was by this time the hot name on the lips of Hollywood's more fearful celebrities. He established himself as the security expert who could best neutralize the risk to celebrities from crazed fans and stalkers. Rejoicing in the title 'threat assessment pioneer' bestowed on him by the approving Dr Park Dietz, the psychiatrist for the John W. Hinckley Jr. prosecution, he became the spearhead of a new modernized security industry serving the famous. This new industry, which even spawned its own trade journal, *Risk Management* magazine, went far beyond the traditional role of supplying bodyguards to shield the famous from the fervent on public occasions. Gavin de Becker advised them on domestic alarm systems and how to create strongrooms in their homes that intruders could not penetrate. He told them to vary their daily routines constantly, so no stalker or would-be kidnapper could plan around their regular schedules. He stressed the desirability of keeping a low profile wherever possible; one of his tips was to change tell-tale, easily identifiable personalized licence plates on their cars.

One might feel this was stoking the flames of paranoia for profit, but in fairness de Becker was merely exploiting a buyers' market. He boasted of 120 'major media figures' among his clients, and though he invariably declined to disclose their identities, their names and his frequently came up in court cases that hinged on the stalking of and criminal intrusion upon celebrities who included Madonna, Robert Redford, Cher, Tina Turner, Dolly Parton. Michael J. Fox, another victim, said of him: 'Gavin and his staff provide what amounts to a Secret Service for famous people.'

Fox's political analogy turned out to be predictive. De Becker's business expanded to include government agencies, including the FBI, the CIA and the Supreme Court, as well as a smattering of *Fortune 500* companies. And he claims to have the world's largest database of 'threatening and obsessive communications', consisting of more than 300,000 pieces of material. Celebrities became his friends; it was at his house that George Harrison is strongly believed to have died.

Some stalkers go to extraordinary lengths to hunt their prey, often giving up any semblance of a normal life. In extreme cases, they quit their jobs or cut themselves off from family members who fail to understand their obsession. Gavin de Becker has known stalkers to take jobs with phone companies in order to obtain the addresses and numbers of their star targets, or talk themselves into work as security guards on the sets of films starring their favourite celebrity.

Nancy Hooper, a writer for *Risk Management*, quotes a US National Institute of Justice statistic that there have been as many attacks on public figures in the last twenty years as in the previous 175. She goes on: 'In fact, an estimated 150,000 people in the United States today are pursuing some kind of unwarranted and inappropriate contact with famous people – and that doesn't include the cases that are kept under wraps.' The figure of 150,000 sounds astonishingly high; but if divided by ten, it would still seem alarming.

On a tip-of-the-iceberg basis, there may be something in it. Over a twelve-month period in the writing of this book there were court cases involving the stalking of the following celebrities: Brad Pitt, Jerry Lewis, Ashley Judd, Barbra Streisand, Madonna, Gwyneth Paltrow, Sharon Stone, Nicole Kidman, Jeri Ryan (from the cast of *Star Trek*), Linda Ronstadt, Axl Rose of Guns 'n' Roses, Brooke Shields, radio 'shock-jock' Howard Stern, talk-show host David Letterman and British teenage pop star Billie Piper.

Many of us, if faced with such awful allegations against us in a court of law, might take it into our heads to keep a very low profile indeed. Some of today's stalkers feel no such bashfulness. Matthew E. Hooker, against whom Nicole Kidman obtained a restraining order in 2001, discusses the stalking accusations against him in detail on his own web site, where he also contributes a poem he wrote for her. He admits he had been trying to interest her in a film script he had written, called *The Activist*. But Hooker also admits he tried to date her, 'since there was flirtation, chemistry and mutual interest on both sides when we met'. He is also using his web site to advance his candidacy for US President in 2004, and sets out his policies in lavish detail: 'I have always believed it was my destiny to be President,' he notes in his introduction to his manifesto.

Some fans go even further, taking their obsessions to macabre lengths. The Icelandic pop singer Bjork was stalked by an American named Ricardo Lopez. In 1996 he sent a letter bomb to her London home, which was intercepted by British police. Lopez then filmed himself on video blowing his brains out with a pistol. Playing in the background was a Bjork song called 'I Miss You'.

This is a long way removed from blurting out 'I really love your work!' At the Ricardo Lopez level, of course, we are talking about severe personality disorders. And yet it must be admitted that severely delusional fans are simply exhibiting extreme responses to the false promises that celebrity holds out. If the public personae of famous people (be they actors, pop stars, sportsmen or politicians) involve allure, stress their attractiveness and suggest possible intimacy, it is hardly surprising that fans will be hooked. And eventually, after all that emotional investment in a celebrity, they may want to stake their claim to a part of what appears to be on offer.

Rarely has this uncomfortable truth been expressed so eloquently as in Stephen Sondheim's blackly comic musical, *Assassins*, which was first staged in 1990. Its characters are a group of people from various historical eras who have tried (sometimes successfully) to assassinate the President of the United States. Sondheim couches the act of assassination as a potentially redemptive act: a means for America's losers, the rejected and oppressed, to claim their 'piece of the pie', their share of the American Dream. Later, the whole cast cluster around the figure of Lee Harvey Oswald, urging him to grasp immortality by killing President Kennedy.

Sondheim and his librettist John Weidman were simply pointing out a hugely uncomfortable truth: that psychopaths who resolve to turn their inner neuroses into outward action against public figures can indeed reap the same recognition accorded to celebrities. John W. Hinckley Jr. and Mark David Chapman became household names as a result of their attempts on the lives of President Reagan and John

Lennon. Serial killer Ted Bundy achieved worldwide fame. So did the murderer Gary Gilmore, who posthumously achieved the extra cachet of a weighty biography by Norman Mailer, no less. Four decades on, all Americans know of Lee Harvey Oswald; fourteen decades on, most of them know of John Wilkes Booth too.

Yet hostility towards famous people can manifest itself in perfectly sane if somewhat tasteless ways. One is the 'death pool' or 'ghoul pool', in which people place small bets on which famous person will die next. Some offices have ongoing death pools organized by employees, and at any one time there are hot favourites: usually the very elderly (Bob Hope, Katharine Hepburn) or those who live a wild lifestyle (Robert Downey Jr., Eminem, Keith Richards of the Rolling Stones).

I first encountered death pools in 1982, when John Belushi was found dead in the Chateau Marmont Hotel in Los Angeles, having injected himself with a cocaine–heroin cocktail; it emerged that there was a death pool run by employees of a major Hollywood studio in which the errant Belushi was a long-time hot favourite. (On his death, his close friend Robin Williams, then another drug abuser who was with Belushi in his last days, became the celebrity most likely to succumb.) Now there are death pools everywhere. A Pittsburgh radio station has an ongoing ghoul pool on its drive-time morning show. There was a short-lived website called stiffs.com, which invited participants to 'go for the gold that lies in the back teeth of the rich and feeble'.

One could read into the existence of death pools a healthy disregard for status, a recognition that however inflated a reputation people have in their lifetimes, even the most celebrated must eventually die.

That theory would hold water were it not for a particularly morbid fascination surrounding celebrity deaths, be they natural, violent or suspicious. An enterprising company in Los Angeles caters for those of a ghoulish disposition by organizing tours of locations where stars met their deaths controversially or unexpectedly. And in truth there is an element of seedy, guilty glamour in a startling star-related death, whether it's Belushi overdosing on junk in the Marmont; James Dean on Highway 41, recklessly smashing his silver Porsche into another vehicle at eighty-five miles an hour; or the hapless, obscure English actress Peg Entwistle, who finally clinched her fame by throwing herself off the fifty-foot Hollywoodland sign in 1932.

From the fans' point of view, something odd happens when a favourite star dies. Initially, there is often a widespread, spontaneous outpouring of grief, as witnessed after the deaths of Rudolph Valentino, James Dean, Elvis Presley and more recently and most notably of Diana, Princess of Wales. In the short term, fans tend to scour the facts of dead stars' lives for evidence of martyrdom: any suggestion that they were driven or hounded to their deaths is gratefully pounced upon. But over a longer term, another factor comes into play. In a curious way, death cements a contract between celebrity and fan that becomes immutable. It's as if a kind of resolution and peace finally descends on an inherently fraught, unsatisfying relationship.

With premature deaths, what remains is an image of unsullied, perfect youth. Dean was only twenty-four when he died, and stays in the collective memory as a troubled, rebellious, eternally doomed young man. No matter that his mannered and limited acting style would have caught him out before too much longer: his death made him a legend. The power of Princess Diana's memory is also enhanced by the fact she was in her physical prime when she met her death, as evidenced by an exquisite photo spread in *Vanity Fair* and a series of pictures aboard the yacht of her boyfriend Dodi Fayed that even made the paparazzi who took them look talented.

There is a terrible poignancy about a famous person cut down at the height of their powers. Fans justifiably speculate over what their future careers might have held. In the field of music, Buddy Holly, Jimi Hendrix and Hank Williams were among those who departed early, with rich veins of talent unmined. Even now Jim Morrison's fans gather earnestly each year in the Paris cemetery to leave flowers and messages at his grave, though it's clear he was pretty much a spent force. Part of their homage is to his indelible image as a young man: beautiful, slim, reckless and yet to be befuddled by drugs and liquor.

But youth and beauty at the time of death are not necessary components of posthumous fan worship. A minor example is country singer Jim Reeves, who died in a 1964 plane crash, shortly before his fortieth birthday. By that point Reeves looked middle-aged and hardly charismatic; but then he had looked that way since his mid-twenties.

This did not prevent his post-death recording career going into overdrive. Elvis Presley is the prime proof of this thesis. By his death in 1977 he was a bloated parody of his former self, and the intrigue of his live shows lay largely in whether Elvis would remember the lyrics or indeed whether he could keep from collapsing on stage. Given the first three extraordinary years of his career – in which he single-handedly turned twentieth-century popular music upside down – Presley's was a long, slow fall from grace. Yet not even a series of truly rotten films and a fifteen-year period in which he only sporadically reclaimed his old magic on record worked against him in death. The Elvis cult lives on today with a sizeable army of generally untalented impersonators, alleged sightings in suburban supermarkets and do-it-yourself stores, and in the minds of deluded women who insist the King is alive and has recently ravished them.

Dead celebrities: what perfect objects for adoration. No more arrogant rebuffs for fans, no disappointments that famous lives are being squandered in unsuitable behaviour. Instead, stars' images stay deep-frozen at the point of death. Forever alluring and acquiescent, they never again pose the risk of shunning, through unavailability or hostility, the one person on earth who truly understood them.

5
The Media

RULE FIVE:
Famous people are now just recurring bit-part players in a huge, constantly unfolding media drama

The excesses of fan worship may titillate, amuse and occasionally horrify us, but it is almost more intriguing to examine fandom on a less fevered level, as it is expressed by millions of average people. Why do so many of us feel a need to monitor the lives of celebrities so closely? It is entirely logical that we would enjoy someone's singing, appreciate an individual's acting ability or marvel at the sensitivity of a concert pianist; we might rejoice at the benefits to mankind resulting from the researches of a scientific pioneer, or salute an international statesman who strives tirelessly for peace. Yet these various shades of admiration are at least founded in some exceptional achievement or skill. Why do we also need to know intimate secrets of their private lives? More pertinently, why do we need to know about the lives of people who have little discernible skill or no achievements worth mentioning?

The astonishing increase in the last century in the number of people deemed famous (even if only for being famous) suggests a gap that was waiting to be filled. Social commentators have pointed to the decline of religion in some Western countries, and to a relatively new worldwide social mobility that hastens the disintegration of hitherto stable, cohesive communities. I wonder whether interest in the lives of celebrities does not satisfy an older, more primal need: the need to be told stories.

Few people without a professional interest in fame and its allied industries are so obsessed by a single celebrity or by celebrities in general to the extent that their lives are furnished with meaning as a result; for the vast majority of us, fame is no substitute for a system of religious beliefs. Nor is it clear that most people (in developed countries at least) mourn the loss of old-fashioned communities, the sort of places that can be typified by neighbours chatting across a garden fence. People have found ways to feel affiliated via new forms of community, whether through the means of e-mail, Internet chat rooms or mobile phones.

But there certainly appears to be a need for narrative in our lives, for stories that tell us, to put it crudely, how to live. This need goes back thousands of years. One thinks of men and women from primeval times, sitting around a fire outside their caves at night, being regaled with stories about the gods, and in later years about legendary earth-bound heroes. What are these early stories, if not exemplars of desirable or undesirable behaviour and guides of how to overcome the problems life raises? These days, of course, we look to novels and biographies, to television drama, the cinema and theatre for our narrative. But buying a book is a discrete event, as is attending a play; these are narratives consumed in an isolated instance. Television provides regular doses of narrative drama, usually spooned out in weekly doses, with the notable exception of the more frequent, sometimes even daily, soap operas.

But for a continuous drip-feed of narrative, it is the media to which we largely look, whether TV news or daily newspapers. The media have latched on to the fact that 'news' about celebrities represents a form of nourishing narrative to their consumers; famous people are thus treated as recurring bit-part players in a huge, constantly unfolding drama, and we can monitor their fluctuating fortunes, career upheavals, romances and marriage break-ups. New stories about them are constantly shaped by the sense of an ongoing narrative about them; reports inevitably remind readers or viewers of the background and context of their lives in which these new plot twists occur.

The formula used to be rather simple, and could be summarized by the phrase 'build 'em up, knock 'em down'. This was shorthand for a process that begins when the media over-enthusiastically latch on to nascent celebrities, inevitably characterized by the word 'hot'. The tone of reporting in this early courtship period is often breathless and flattering, and outlines how the new kids in town negotiate the pitfalls of sudden fame, lay to rest any skeletons from the past in their closet, and come to settle on a persona – cheeky, brash, witty, sincere, flippant, shy, flirtatious – that they can employ as a kind of mask in their dealings with the public and media.

This early phase of the relationship with the media remains amiable up until a certain point. It is a point that the media are remarkably astute at judging; a point at which new celebrities are comfortably ensconced in their fame, and have had more than their fair share of media attention. It is a point at which the glamour and novelty of their new-found fame starts to wear thin, when they begin to display mild signs of irritation at being constantly in the spotlight, at the endless sense of intrusion, at the lack of privacy. They suddenly seem to act less charmingly, less ingenuously, less gratefully, and incipient signs of boorish or aloof conduct may be observed.

And at this point, the media turn on them. It is judged that the time has come when the public has tired of them (a condition, of course, encouraged by the media's own hyper-enthusiasm) and is now ready to see them get their comeuppance. Most celebrities undergoing this process have no idea that it is about to happen, or why and where the relationship soured. In fact, all that has occurred is that they have moved along fame's conveyor belt: they are being shunted aside to make way for a new raft of fresh, bright-eyed, compliant celebrities about to undergo the same process.

The most extraordinary example of this tendency I can recall happened in England to the then husband-and-wife acting team Kenneth Branagh and Emma Thompson. At first, they seemed an unstoppable, gilded young couple. He, as actor, director and film producer, was justifiably hailed as the new Laurence Olivier in the wake of his Oscar-nominated success *Henry V*. She was sharp, witty, formidably bright and every bit his equal as an actor, winning an Oscar for *Howards End*, and being nominated for *The Remains of the Day* and *Sense and Sensibility*.

The couple married in a glittering ceremony at Cliveden, a sumptuous stately home. Branagh embarked on writing an autobiography while only twenty-eight years old, though not purely for reasons of personal vanity; the advance from the book would help fund future projects for his production company Renaissance. Still, he and Thompson showed every sign of enjoying their fame, even revelling in it. They had a genuine talent for self-publicity, and did not indulge in displays of sham modesty. Yet they allowed themselves to become over-exposed; at one point, around 1990, it seemed impossible to open a British newspaper without being confronted by pictures of 'Ken and Em' gushing at each other. Of course, they were proud of their achievements, and assumed many people in Britain might feel the same way.

In this, they over-estimated the British press, how swiftly it can become sated by the omnipresence of successful people, and how it enjoys seeing the mighty humbled. Branagh and Thompson were kicked around mercilessly, hauled over the coals for being precious, self-regarding, and for getting above themselves. They were damned as over-ambitious, creatures of Thatcherism's worst aspects. Failing to see it coming, they felt wounded. Thompson later admitted that the strategy of trumpeting their achievements backfired. 'Given the chance to do it again,' she told me, 'I wouldn't do that much publicity. I'd be much more choosy. But what I found really repellent was that some papers, having mostly said I was OK before I married Ken, then said oh, she gets work because of her husband. I thought, boy, is that ever mean-spirited. Not to mention sexist.'

Branagh, trying to sound equable, once explained to me how he saw the process of fame as invigilated by the British media: 'I know on the whole the press are not three-headed monsters. I know a lot of the people who have written ghastly things about me. But I think in Britain you go through a cycle – you get discovered, then maybe you get a little too popular or too lauded. Then another cycle sets in: they're happy with you, because other people have come along that they can do it to.

'In a strange way the press are very familiar with me. I'm referred to as "our Ken". There's a kind of paternal thing that's strangely affectionate. Maybe it's the nature of this country: it's so small and insular that you go through a kind of family relationship, and get told off a lot.'

Still, the experience clearly stung them both. They split up in 1995, citing demanding and conflicting work schedules as a contributory factor, and both of them have since lived resolutely low-key lives. Branagh now gives interviews reluctantly, but only about specific work projects, and on the strict understanding that his private life is not discussed. Thompson adopted an even lower profile, cutting back on acting assignments and concentrating on screenwriting. Her boyfriend, actor Greg Wise, moved into her house, and they had a child together. Thompson now walks around the streets of her London neighbourhood in ordinary street clothes, without a trace of make-up, and rarely suffers intrusion from the public.

The actor Bruce Willis told novelist Jay McInerney in a 1995 *Esquire* magazine interview: 'There's only four basic stories they can write about you. One: you hit the scene. Two: you peak. Three: you bomb. And four: you come back.' But celebrity narratives can be more complex, as exemplified by the Branagh–Thompson saga. Here was a glittering young couple who rose fast, achieved solid success, suffered setbacks in terms of public popularity, then split up to make separate lives for themselves. There is enough material in their story so far to serve as a background for any number of intriguing future narrative twists: if the career of one outstrips the other, for example, or if they ever work together again.

And yet Willis, perhaps unwittingly, hit on something. There is indeed something archetypal about the rise–peak–bust–comeback scenario that he describes. It follows a familiar narrative pattern, that of hero myths passed down to successive generations for thousands of years.

The key name here is Joseph Campbell (1904–87), the scholar, writer, teacher and eminent authority on mythology, best known for his classic works *The Hero With A Thousand Faces* and *The Mask of God*. He took the view that certain basic hero myths have long been embedded in the histories of most cultures. In *The Hero With A Thousand Faces*, he traces the outline of such a hero myth: 'A hero ventures forth from the world of common day into a region of supernatural wonder; fabulous forces are there encountered, and a decisive victory is won; the hero comes back from this mysterious adventure with the power to bestow boons on his fellow man.'

The story of Jesus Christ, though related with slight variations in each of the four New Testament gospels, conforms to this outline. Christ grew up in humble surroundings, started to perform miracles and attracted followers. He spent a metaphorical forty days in the wilderness, was tempted by Satan, but overcame temptation. Though his life ended with his crucifixion, his resurrection became the foundation for the dissemination of his teachings.

Campbell is an influential name in modern-day narratives; one of his leading acolytes is film-maker George Lucas whose *Star Wars*, the story of the young hero Luke Skywalker, closely follows the archetypal heroic myths outlined by Campbell. For about a decade after the huge success of *Star Wars*, it seemed that half the screenwriters in Hollywood were desperately (and tiresomely) cleaving to Campbell's ideas about narrative structure.

Today, oddly, this same narrative structure is used as a template from which stories about celebrities can be shaped. The media connive in this; they may not consciously strive to concoct hero myths, but they frame new developments in the lives of celebrities as new episodes in a compelling ongoing narrative. The status of hero was once reserved for people of real achievements; today's heroes, lacking achievements of substance, instead have their private lives and careers moulded by the media and their own handlers to resemble a diluted version of a hero myth.

This moulding takes place in circles far loftier than the entertainment business. During one of his successful Presidential campaigns, Bill Clinton's handlers dubbed him the Comeback Kid. In truth, Clinton was only rebounding from some not very impressive numbers in public opinion polls, but no matter, the catchy phrase helped enrich his biography, marking him as someone who had suffered setbacks but emerged a stronger man. Earlier, during the campaign that finally saw him elected to the White House, Richard Nixon made great play of his wilderness years and their implied contribution to building his character.

For a celebrity, especially a mature male, it's an appealing image: a man who has been knocked about and bruised a little by life, but keeps going, thanks to some stubborn inner fortitude. The self-serving lyrics to the song 'My Way', a latter-day signature for Frank Sinatra, encapsulate this image perfectly. It helps for famous people to admit to vulnerability, or periods of wretchedness and despair in their lives, because they provide a springboard for a triumphant comeback. This serves two purposes: the troughs in their life make them seem fallible, and the media, quickly tiring of infallible celebrities, look for ways to cut them down to size. But equally important, life's vagaries provide a continuing narrative in lives that at closer inspection might seem to be monotonously successful and content.

Yet some of these stories about the famous enduring tough times are hard to take seriously. It is conventional wisdom that film director Quentin Tarantino rescued John Travolta's career by casting him in the 1994 hit movie *Pulp Fiction*; Travolta's career, it was implied, had died since his huge movie successes from the late 1970s, *Saturday Night Fever* and *Grease*. But he was hardly starving. In 1989, he signed up to star in an innocuous, critically ignored little comedy, *Look Who's Talking*, about a baby who talked. As it was a low-budget film, he agreed to a modest salary, but asked for a share of the profits. The picture cost $7 million to produce and grossed $450 million worldwide. Travolta walked away with $150 million, and also earned vast sums from the film's two sequels. He is one of the world's richest film actors; he owns three private jets. But because the *Look Who's Talking* films were largely neglected by the media, Travolta was provided with a chance to position himself as an underdog. 'When I got hired by Quentin, I did not have a real awareness of how totally uncool I had become,' he has said. It was not recorded whether he was laughing up his sleeve as he said it.

But it is smarter to portray oneself as someone who has fallen victim to fluctuations in fortunes; it makes one appear more likeable. Actor Michael Caine likes it to be known that he has suffered from being an outsider; born into a poor working-class London family, he has long claimed that British critics underrate him and that London's theatrical establishment view him with disdain. Some outsider. Caine is immensely wealthy; the Queen has knighted him; he has won an Oscar and been nominated for one several times. Yet he complains that in Britain 'I'm regarded as an extremely lucky cockney yobbo who managed to be in the right place at the right time. There's no sense that I've ever learned to do anything or that I do it with skill.'

Caine has also conducted a public love–hate relationship with Britain. He spent eight years living in Los Angeles as a vocal tax exile, then quietly returned home. Yet he once complained to me of a major misperception about him, an assumption he did not live in Britain. People are entitled to change their views and opinions with the passing years, but Caine's volatility and mood swings also provide him with a narrative, portraying himself as a cheeky but talented underdog who holds a justified grudge.

Entertainers frequently style themselves as survivors, a showbiz cliché that detracts from the power of the word, and usually means only that their careers or lives have dipped and peaked in a way familiar to most people. Yet how ruthlessly the famous milk this formulation, how easily a comeback can be framed as stirring and dramatic. Look at how often a has-been returns to glory and wins a surprise Oscar, which then also becomes an award for a long, distinguished, insufficiently acknowledged career. Think of Henry Fonda in 1981, winning the Academy Award for *On Golden Pond*, with every Oscar voter aware of the fact he was terminally ill.

Another self-serving song, Elton John's 'I'm Still Standing', could serve as the official anthem for this grisly tendency. It is a painfully easy device for eliciting free publicity: consider Sinatra, who announced his retirement from recording and performing several times, then kept returning. He even got an album title out of it – *Ol' Blue Eyes is Back!* – though it is doubtful anyone had hitherto called him Ol' Blue Eyes. The whole exercise was transparently fake, but each time Sinatra 'retired', it was an opportunity for writing gushing retrospectives about his career. And each time he changed his mind the media, seizing on the narrative possibilities opened up by his comebacks, trumpeted them as welcome events that warranted the public's immense gratitude.

Battles with various forms of addiction are another valuable means of sustaining a narrative about a celebrity. Robert Downey Jr., more famous for his problems with substance abuse than his acting ability, repeatedly made headlines each time he fell from grace, a problem to which he contributed by telling various judges in a number of courts that he was determined to get help and resist the lure of his addictions.

Serial monogamy is another easy device for maintaining one's own personal narrative in public. In this regard, Elizabeth Taylor has no peer. Her many marriages have been tracked avidly by the press since the early 1950s, and she fanned the flames of her own publicity by making her differences with successive husbands known to the press. When things got really bad, she would succumb to mysterious illnesses and be rushed to hospital. (If we feel tempted to sneer at how uniquely in thrall to celebrity trivia we are today, it is instructive to look back to that time when Taylor lured Eddie Fisher from his wife Debbie Reynolds, and subsequently dumped Fisher for Richard Burton. The extent of the media coverage was extraordinary, even by present-day standards.)

Eventually Taylor's husbands became increasingly less plausible: John Warner, a minor Republican senator; a strapping builder named Larry Fortensky. Finally she appeared to tire of the marriage game, settling into a third, less sensational career as a one-woman focal point for Aids charities. But by this time the media were used to reporting each new development in her life, so they reported that as well. Taylor's epic public narrative now stretches back a full fifty years, and one needs to be that old to recall even dimly what it was that first made her famous, the fact that she was once an impressive film actress.

From the outset, it was clear that Taylor's story was one that could run and run; her exploits were always going to be sufficiently outrageous to fill column inches over several decades. There was never any need for the media to sit in judgement on Liz, or manipulate her life and career. All that was needed was to sit back, watch her in action and report it in detail.

These days, celebrities who look to have a shorter potential shelf life receive harsher treatment. It was once the case, as Willis pointed out, that new celebrities were subjected to a 'build 'em up, knock 'em down' scenario: 'you hit the scene, you peak, you bomb and then you come back'. This process appears to have telescoped in recent years, as if the attention spans of viewers and readers interested in celebrity were not already short enough. Obvious victims include those naïve unfortunates who receive a taste of fame through exposing themselves on reality TV shows. The media cast an eye over them, and scent blood.

When the talent in question shows signs of longevity, the media, equally shamefully, can take the opposite course. After her departure from the Spice Girls, singer Geri Halliwell initially struggled with her solo career as it seemed the four remaining members of the group would eclipse her. Her handlers twice released stories, of dubious veracity, about romances – one with singer Robbie Williams, and one with the British disc jockey Chris Evans. Both stories were timed to run on the eve of release of new records by Halliwell. The British media might have had doubts about the authenticity of her romances, they even knew that Halliwell, Williams and Evans were all handled by the same publicity company, but the stories ran anyway. Halliwell's records duly charted, the 'romances' swiftly and not so mysteriously died. The job was done. Nobody felt sufficiently enraged to complain.

A new phrase was coined for romances such as this. They are now known as 'event relationships', and they have a noble lineage; Hollywood studio publicists were often known to hint coyly at romances between their leading stars, hints that were inevitably presented as facts in the press. This was a neat way of publicizing their latest films; one recalls Warren Beatty's fling with Madonna when they acted together in his 1990 film *Dick Tracy*. Their event relationship ended some time around the film's opening weekend. On a few occasions, the ploy has helped divert public attention from the homosexuality of a leading man; in 1955, Rock Hudson allowed himself to be talked into an unhappy 'show marriage' to one Nancy Gates. It was somehow fitting that she was the secretary to his agent.

Headlines about event relationships tend to have only a short-term effect, though they have their uses: selling newspapers and filling gaps in TV news programmes for a day or so. But the media prefer stories with a much longer life; stories about celebrities that run and run (Frank Rich of the *New York Times* has coined the word 'mediathon' for such stories) represent a kind of gold dust. Why? Because they feed on themselves. Talk about a need for narrative: if such a story has the potential to get a whole nation talking (as Princess Diana's death did in Britain and elsewhere, and both the O. J. Simpson trial and the Clinton–Lewinsky scandal did in the US) it becomes a small industry in its own right: it is developed, milked and manipulated, and gives rise to all kinds of new angles, editorializing and comment, much of it gratuitous. Mediathons fill space on a news page and airtime on television. Put crudely, they are good for business.

They are also distorting. People at the centre of these stories have characters effectively created for them by the media, to sustain a lengthy narrative and maximize the entertainment value of their stories to the public. But what happens when a story fails to conform to a narrative the media wish to shape? The results are sometimes not pleasant to witness. In Britain, the TV quiz show *Who Wants To Be A Millionaire?* had run for more than a year and achieved great popularity without any contestant winning £1 million. The show's huge rating success was given extra thrust by the support of the country's tabloid press, which covered it extensively.

But when in 2000 the first contestant finally answered all fifteen questions correctly and won the £1 million, media rejoicing was muted. Judith Keppel did not fit the narrative the press wanted from a winner. She was from a desirable part of London, a divorced middle-aged woman with a quiet, reserved voice that suggested an upper middle-class upbringing. On meeting the media, she behaved with decorous restraint. She would not disclose in detail how she would spend the money, and indeed implied her life might not change radically. She also declined to strike jubilant poses for the cameras; not for her the obligatory shot in the Jacuzzi, brandishing a glass of champagne in one hand and a wad of banknotes in the other.

Within twenty-four hours the tabloids had turned against her. It was discovered that she was a distant relative of Prince Charles's consort Camilla Parker Bowles, which somehow made her win unfair, and immediately she was too posh to be a good story. Despite Kepple's protestations that she lived rather modestly, the image she presented suggested otherwise. The tabloids deemed her an unsuitable winner, and damned *Who Wants To Be A Millionaire?* as an elitist show, though its selection criteria are clearly random. (These charges resurfaced the following year when a London banker, who really was wealthy and owned two houses, won the £1 million.)

What the tabloids really wanted was the right narrative. The ideal winners would be poor, working-class, from a provincial town, in a menial job. On the show, they would behave humbly and a little haltingly under the cameras' glare, while betraying glimpses of quiet, unforced charm. On winning, they would declare their intention to spend most of the money on material possessions way beyond their reach before their win, with a substantial sum put aside to pay for a relative with a rare disease to travel abroad for an expensive cure. They would be compliant to all media requests, jump for joy and punch the air at photographers' behest. Ideally, they would pass the next couple of years extravagantly spending themselves back into poverty; and the press would follow them every step of the way.

In short, what the press wanted was Viv Nicholson. She was a blonde, attractive, forthright Yorkshire working-class housewife whose second husband won a fortune on the pools in 1961. Her reaction was to tell the media: 'I'm going to spend, spend, spend,' a quote that came back to haunt her. The couple bought a huge home on a hill overlooking their old, small terraced house. She bought a fur coat. Together they bought a huge American car with fins, the sort Elvis Presley might have owned. All too predictably, their money ran out, and the rest of her life was characterized by alcohol, bankruptcy and no less than five subsequent marriages. Unwittingly Viv Nicholson provided the prototypical narrative for the person of humble origins who is 'lucky' enough to get rich quickly. Judith Keppel could not begin to compete.

Even if Kepple's moment of fame was not quite of the kind she would have wanted, most of the journalists writing critically about her would be aghast at the notion that there was any personal animosity towards her. After all, she got the publicity. There is a widespread notion among journalists, even some extremely thoughtful ones, that all publicity is good publicity, that attaining fame is automatically a good thing, almost irrespective of circumstance. One sees why they think this way: fame is a commodity, a currency, a lubricant that keeps the presses rolling, justifies their work and perpetuates the media as a flourishing industry. Journalists are cynical, often rightly so, about famous people who demand privacy as a right, but eagerly seek publicity when it benefits them.

Still, there are celebrities who genuinely view fame as a mixed blessing, and the media as a creature that almost wilfully misunderstands them. I once met the actor John Cusack on a film set in Calgary, Canada, where he talked at length about the pros and cons of fame. He articulated particularly strong feelings, because the day before the local newspaper reported that he had been seen in town dining with actress Neve Campbell.

'It's fine,' he said. 'I'm pretty lucky, because if you're considered a movie star you have a much better shot at getting your film out there. So I can go and promote my movies on David Letterman strenuously.

If I like the film I'll do it, even though I don't like the talk shows. I don't like the personal questions they ask.

'Even these journalists in Calgary who came out here on set, all they wanted to do is ask about who I was dating. Then they started writing I was dating someone. That's the part I don't like. They can't imagine you wouldn't be eager to get press on every aspect of your life. And if you did have dinner with an actress, well, you're a movie star, you must be dating. And they think, well, if *I* was dating her, I'd want everyone to know it. They can't imagine you'd say your private life is not for sale. I can't think of one good reason to answer that question.'

Cusack claimed he has even advised fellow actors and friends never to discuss their private lives. 'I tell them, don't talk about that stuff, all you're doing is selling socks or cosmetics. No one gives a shit about who you're dating or who you slept with. Or how you feel about who you used to date. No one cares. Yet they do it again and again.

'I maintain that every couple who uses their union to promote their film or TV career is doomed to fail. If you go on a talk show and profess your love for someone, or talk in print about what you're trying to do together, you can count down the days to the divorce.'

He has a point. In media circles, there has been much talk of 'the curse of *Hello!* magazine', which alludes to the number of couples who profess undying devotion in the magazine's pages, but are found to have served divorce papers almost before the issue hits the newsstands.

Yet even if Cusack is right about the ludicrous aspects of fame, it also has its uses for those celebrities who fall foul of the law. The televised O. J. Simpson trial was played out not only in a Los Angeles courtroom, but also in the court of American public opinion; several TV stations offered day-by-day commentary on Simpson's demeanour, and the implications of fresh daily evidence on his likely guilt or innocence. Public opinion on whether or not he had murdered his wife was regularly polled, as if this was not so much a criminal trial, but more a popularity contest. Simpson, a man accustomed to being in the public eye and the recipient of acting lessons, conducted himself soberly and gravely in court. He looked good. It was possible to detect in the public mood – and the reporting of the trial – an unspoken wish that he be found not guilty. It was as if fame had thrown a protective blanket around him, and his celebrity placed him in a kind of moral vacuum where he was not to be judged as other men. And of course, when he walked free, the media were free to continue their long, detailed, gripping narrative about him and his post-trial activities – an option that would have been denied them had he served jail time.

Michael Jackson is another celebrity who appears to exist in this blessed moral vacuum. It is known that charges were pressed against him alleging molestation of an under-age boy, and that those charges were settled without a case ever coming to court. But the media are oddly amnesiac on this score: when Jackson visited England in 2001, he addressed the Oxford Union about the need to nurture and protect children. No one pointed out the dubious nature of this connection, nor did they raise the charge that Jackson was living in an odd, hermetically sealed world of such delusion and denial that he genuinely could not make the connection himself. Again, the media seemed to be conspiring to protect a public figure in whom they saw much future mileage. Jackson is an eccentric figure, and the media have great sport with him; they report his peculiar, ever-evolving appearance, his pet llamas, his fondness for wearing an oxygen mask in public. As such, his is a compelling ongoing narrative. Perhaps there is a realization that if the darker side of his life were probed thoroughly, it would mean the end of his public career. End of narrative. Bad for business.

6

Everybody's Famous

RULE SIX:
In future, anyone will appear on television if they want it badly enough

Shortly before his death in 1987, the great mythology scholar and writer Joseph Campbell bemoaned the estrangement of modern man from the myths and legends that had sustained our ancestors. 'One of our problems today is that we are not well acquainted with the literature of the spirit,' he said. 'We're interested in the news of the day and the problems of the hour.' In a series of interviews with American broadcaster Bill Moyers (some of which, tellingly, took place at *Star Wars* producer George Lucas's Skywalker Ranch) Campbell voiced a need for new 'myths that will identify the individual not with his local group but his planet'. He attributed sectarian bloodshed in such trouble spots as the Middle East and Northern Ireland to 'the failure of religion to meet the modern world', and noted that down the ages there has been a gradual diminution of our cultural heroes.

This is a commonly heard complaint. The psychotherapist Nan Beecher-Moore believes the modern obsession with celebrities fulfils a need for some folk narrative in our lives. 'I think there is a loss of any relationship to myths and legends of our culture,' she says. 'What happened to our understanding of those legends and myths?'

It is certainly true that stories passed around in ancient civilizations had lofty themes. They had to do with the exploits of gods. In the medieval era, audiences were enthralled by the exploits of kings and warriors. Shakespeare wrote of monarchs and people of low birth, sometimes within the same play, but sought to establish some universality within his characters – idealized versions of his audience. With the arrival of the novel in the late eighteenth century, heroes increasingly became archetypically ordinary people.

In the last hundred years we have looked to political heroes

(Churchill, Gandhi, Kennedy, Mandela) and increasingly to entertainment figures, especially film stars and pop artists. Campbell conceded this last point, referring to the movie theatre as 'a special temple' and to films as 'magical': 'The person you are looking at is also somewhere else at the same time. That is a condition of the god.' Maybe so, though it is a startling progression from Zeus and Aphrodite to Tom Cruise and Julia Roberts.

As it turned out, the progression had some way further to go. At least Cruise and Roberts have a skill; they know how to act appealingly in movies. And at least it took them some years to worm their way into the public consciousness. Quite what Joseph Campbell would have made of the cataclysmic changes that inverted the values of fame and cultural heroism in the year 2000 must remain open to conjecture. This was the first year of 'reality TV', with shows such as the phenomenally successful *Big Brother* in Britain and *Survivor* in the US featuring casts of non-famous people seemingly chosen for their ordinariness. Let us leave that word 'seemingly' aside for a while, and examine the premise of *Big Brother*.

Ten people, most of them in their twenties, were chosen to live in a specially built house in which every room was under surveillance from hidden cameras twenty-four hours a day. They simply had to interact with each other, carry out more or less amusing tasks set by the programme's producers, and at the end of each week nominate two among them who would be expelled from the house. The viewing audience would then cast their own votes from the nominations, so one person at a time was ejected. After everyone else was eliminated, the winner would receive a £70,000 cash prize. The show was aimed primarily at an audience in their teens and twenties, who watched enthralled as the house members argued, made up, formed cliques, sulked, hugged, flung most of their clothes off, shouted, jumped into hot tubs, flirted – and talked. They talked incessantly at a consistently banal level, their minds rarely troubled by anything so complex as an idea. Soon viewers found themselves rooting for one occupant to survive the elimination process, and forming an antipathy towards some of the others, an emotion they could satisfy by voting for their dismissal. The skill of *Big Brother* was in the way it cued its audience to seek out their favourites in the house. Not someone brighter, or more talented, or more attractive, or more dazzling in conversation: just someone like them, someone with whom they felt they might get along.

In Britain, the show became a significant cultural event, and during its first season, in the summer of 2000, it came to dominate public discourse, especially among its target audience, to an extraordinary extent. The virtues and flaws of all contestants were analysed earnestly; everyone seemed to have an opinion about who they wanted to win and who they wished to see eliminated next. The occupants of the house became the most gossiped-about people in Britain. Tabloid (and some broadsheet) papers began running features about them, their backgrounds, their personal lives, and the whole *Big Brother* phenomenon. Older columnists huffed and puffed about the series, its monopolistic stranglehold on the nation's attention, and its value as an indication the whole of civilization was going straight to hell. And what happened? The house-sitters became famous, temporarily elbowing aside 'real' celebrities who could actually do something, even if only movie acting or singing a pop song.

This was foreseeable. The sort of people who applied to go on the show tended to be their own biggest fans, and had calculated beforehand that such prolonged, intense exposure on television might help viewers love them almost as much as they loved themselves. Even more crucially, airing their personalities on *Big Brother* might prove a short cut to long-term, if unspecified fame; nine of the ten contestants in the first season ticked a box marked 'fame and fortune' as a reason for competing. To some viewers the show looked a tedious, draining ordeal: up to nine weeks of incarceration, surrounded by largely irritating, self-absorbed people, while one's every move was being recorded on camera. But the contestants knew better: they saw it as an extended audition that might alter their lives.

Initially, it seemed they might be right, especially towards the end of the first season, when *Big Brother* mania was at its peak. Only three people remained in the house, while the producers had expelled a fourth, an opportunistic, manipulative young man named Nick Bateman for breaches of house etiquette, involving setting other occupants against each other. (For one disorienting week, 'Nasty Nick' was Britain's most talked-about man.)

It was soon apparent in that first season that many contestants had been chosen because they were of a type: outgoing, faintly outrageous, upbeat, reasonably attractive and unembarrassed by flirtation or sexually loaded situations, all of which made them, in professional parlance, 'good television'. They also shared a certain egocentricity; quick to offer loud opinions in any situation, they instinctively knew how to project their personalities for the benefit of the unseen cameras. In brief, they were extrovert bores.

Nichola Holt, a shaven-haired lesbian, attracted notoriety for her apparent inability to keep her clothes on. Caroline O'Shea, a brassy blonde who had once sold marital aids, became infamous for a raucous laugh that might conceivably strip paint from a wall. After the first series, these two made headlines for attending a TV awards ceremony in a state of inebriation, and knocking over a TV presenter, Vanessa Feltz. The incident did much to confirm *Big Brother* contestants as loud-mouthed exhibitionists.

Yet intriguingly the last three occupants to survive were by objective standards the most likeable (or strictly speaking, the least dislikeable). Viewers quickly rejected the ones who most closely represented 'good television', with their tiresome tendency for perpetually brazen behaviour. Craig Phillips, the eventual winner, was an aggressively cheerful but good-hearted builder. Quietly-spoken Darren Ramsay was low-key, almost introspective. Anna Nolan, sensationally billed as a gay ex-trainee nun, was the most thoughtful and intelligent of the bunch.

How did they fare later, those who ticked the 'fame and fortune' box? Indifferently. In terms of contrast between the promise of celebrity and anti-climactic reality, entering the *Big Brother* house as a contestant turned out to be on a par with selection as one of Hugh Hefner's Playmates: it was a one-way ticket to obscurity. Nichola Holt made a record called 'The Game', which peaked at number 72 in the UK charts. (Even the official *Big Brother* website referred to the record as 'her first, and possibly her last'!) With a ghost-writer, Nick Bateman rushed out a book called *How To Be A Right Bastard*, which resolutely remained on bookstore shelves. Anna Nolan landed a job as a presenter on a TV series called *Closure*, but her role was subordinate to Davina McCall, who had hosted *Big Brother*. Melanie Hill undertook travel assignments for *Marie Claire* magazine's UK edition. Winner Craig Phillips put his £70,000 towards a heart-lung transplant in America for Joanne Harris, his best friend's eighteen-year-old cousin. But fame hardly came his way, either. He too released a record, 'At This Time Of Year', timed for the Christmas market. When it failed to sell, the record company cancelled his contract. He landed a stint on a BBC do-it-yourself programme, but real fame eluded him.

The most telling brush with celebrity life was Darren Ramsay's, and it too ended badly. Because he was of Jamaican origin, the charity Christian Aid invited him to visit Kingston, see the work it was doing there for children with Aids, and spread the word in the media. Ramsay found himself emotionally overwhelmed by what he saw. In Mandela Terrace in inner-city Kingston, he came face to face with a five-year-old Jamaican girl lying on a bed, suffering from Aids and cancer. It was too much for him; he cut short his visit and returned home.

This was entirely understandable and predictable. Nothing in his twenty-three years of life had prepared him for any such trauma. Fame was thrust upon him too quickly, and he had no idea how to adapt. In any case, such visits by celebrities to ailing or wounded people carry uncomfortable overtones: no patient needs literally to touch the hem of celebrities' robes, but a suggestion hangs heavy on the air that their mere presence carries with it some healing power. Princess Diana managed to convey this illusion with a real and increasing conviction on visits to hospitals, to children with Aids, and the victims of landmine explosions. But poor Darren Ramsay buckled under the weight of his new, unmerited adulation; an ordinary man, he was unaccustomed to such power and responsibility.

Given that this group of ten were, albeit briefly, the most talked about people in Britain, their demise seems astonishing; they disappeared from the public gaze as quickly as they had encroached upon it. The trajectory of their rise and fall corresponded to a classic arc of fame but speeded up many times over. It was as if everyone but themselves – their handlers, the media, the public – understood that they were ersatz celebrities, disposable, not for keeps. Summer is a notoriously slow season for the media, and 'real' news is thin on the ground; once the midsummer madness of *Big Brother* was over, normal service could be resumed and these people could be forgotten.

This did not prevent a new season of the show in the summer of 2001, which similarly commanded headlines, comment, opinion and gossip. E4, a little-watched British cable TV channel, broadcast live sixteen hours a day from the house, inevitably including long periods when contestants simply slept. This gave it a dubious status. By dint of merely being awake, viewers could be certain that anything going on in their living rooms was more interesting than what was showing on their televisions.

Though *Big Brother*, along with its millions of devoted viewers, has been widely criticized, I think it marks a turning point in the progression of modern fame. Its creators, the Dutch company Endemol, clearly conceived of it differently: they simply foresaw the ripe possibilities of imprisoning ten strangers in one house, and watching how they interacted. While that is certainly part of the show's appeal, the unforeseen element was that viewers would latch on to the contestants like favourite celebrities, rooting for them and urgently discussing them with friends, family and work colleagues. The interaction between the occupants is intriguing in itself, yet because of its unscripted nature, has an improvisatory feel that eludes the most skilfully written soap operas. But when each of the occupants assumes the mantle of celebrity, and then interacts with other 'celebrities' in the house, *Big Brother* comes to resemble a live gossip column, full of feuds, romances, flirtations and arguments. Better yet, it is a gossip column with plot developments that viewers can influence by voting occupants in or out; this factor corresponds neatly to the hostility towards famous people that seems an inevitable component of fans' adoration.

I also wonder if in retrospect *Big Brother* will not be seen as an arena for a newly evolved attitude towards celebrity culture. In Britain, the second series was even more successful than the first, and viewers are rapidly assimilating the notion that the 'celebrities' they adopt for nine short weeks in the summer have a brief shelf life. Yet viewers adopt them anyway, discussing them in a slightly detached, ironic fashion. Is it possible the audience has reached a realization (even if it is one yet to be articulated) that much of our interest in celebrity culture is rooted in a mere love of gossip, rather than in anything intrinsically intriguing about famous figures? Those with vested financial interests in maintaining the appeal of celebrities might be alarmed at the idea of an audience sophisticated enough consciously to regard fame as a disposable commodity; yet to a society increasingly sated with celebrity culture, the prospect might seem delightful.

It might also seem hopelessly optimistic. There are reasons for the proliferation of celebrities in our age, and those reasons are commercial. In the television industry, for instance, the digital revolution promises viewers the choice of dozens of new channels. Those channels have two primary needs: to sustain themselves financially, and to fill their schedules with programming. On the first point, most analysts agree that advertising revenue to television is unlikely to increase sharply, just because more channels are available. Indeed, throughout 2001 in the UK, the fear within the industry was that ad revenues would decrease. So that means more channels will be chasing after a small share of a global sum. And that in turn means their programmes will need to be cheaply made.

Celebrity-related programming is the answer; the famous (or semi-famous) give their time for free because they are plugging their latest product. In return, they meet the new channels' desperate need for programming. Yet because such a small proportion of the population will watch these channels, the celebrities who will agree to appear on them (even in a plugging capacity) are necessarily minor. Forget the A-list of internationally known faces: we're talking about a C or D list, people whose claim to fame is tenuous at best. Gazing mournfully into some metaphorical crystal ball, one can hazard a guess that in the multi-channel future, anyone who badly wants to appear on television has every chance of doing so. Noël Coward once snobbishly remarked that television was for appearing on, not watching; today he might conclude that it is good for neither.

The same problem holds true for print media. New magazines spring up all the time, while more newspapers turn to celebrity interviews or features in an attempt to snare new readers. (Within the media, there is precious little scepticism about, or even discussion of, whether a steady diet of celebrities is the best way to attract an audience or readership.) By necessity, a law of diminishing returns operates: the handful of major celebrities that most TV programmes and publications want to feature confine themselves to a small number of established or successful media outlets. The rest turn to minor celebrities, or *faux* celebrities: that is, people who are famous at one remove.

Faux celebrities are proof that the democratization of fame still has some way to go. They are evidence of a culture that has become so punch-drunk in the face of even secondhand celebrity that it can no longer distinguish what is or is not important.

A manicurist named Jo Carlisle unwittingly underlined this thesis in January 2001, when she made headlines for a few days. She was in the employ of Victoria Beckham, the singer with the Spice Girls, though her designated job title was nothing so humdrum as manicurist. Instead she described herself as Mrs Beckham's nail technician. It emerged that such a person specializes in providing false nails, nail extensions, nail piercings, nail transfers, nail infills, nail art, and a process known as 'nail airbrushing'.

Jo Carlisle became a subject for media discussion after the theft of four suitcases belonging to Victoria Beckham (most press reports carefully identified them as Louis Vuitton suitcases) from Heathrow Airport. And Jo Carlisle, the nail technician in the Beckham entourage, was approached by the thief to arrange for their safe return. A trifling incident, one might think, yet this did not prevent articles about Ms Carlisle from running in several British newspapers. These explained in breathless prose just what being a nail technician entailed. Pictures of Ms Carlisle ran alongside the articles, and it did not hurt that she was blonde and attractive, nor that her own nails looked well tended. The most widely run picture showed her holding a framed photo of Victoria Beckham at an awards ceremony, the singer's hand covering her lower face, thus displaying her nails. She had signed this photo 'To Jo – the nails looked wicked!' And that was the justification for the hoo-ha: Jo Carlisle wasn't famous herself, but she helped to perfect the cuticles of someone who was.

In fairness she was only joining a huge, rapidly-growing crowd of people whose credentials for fame were dubious at best. Traditional entertainers – actors, singers, bandleaders and comedians – found their ranks swelled by the most unlikely people. The term 'supermodel' was coined to justify thousands of column inches and splashy pictures of those models who earned most money. In the 1990s, dozens of them came to be regarded as legitimate celebrities. Recently, fashion magazines have started to take seriously the opinions of stylists – mostly young women whose main job is to stand around at fashion shoots and recordings of pop videos, and murmur to the talent that they're looking good. Chefs have edged into the frame of the celebrity picture in large numbers. Diet advisers began to be taken seriously as personalities. Personal fitness trainers wrote books about their methods and were interviewed on television. Minor socialites (especially that shallow, exasperating breed known in Britain as It Girls), fashion designers, hairdressers and career criminals joined the celebrity fraternity; all one needed to become a *de facto* famous person was an energetic, resourceful publicist.

And even publicists, those puppeteers who manoeuvre the strings of celebrity, became a focus of interest; such hucksters as Pat Kingsley and Peggy Siegel in the US, and Max Clifford and Matthew Freud in the UK, were profiled reverentially in magazines and newspapers that should have known better. They were frequently dubbed 'PR gurus', a fawning, overwrought phrase that ignored any possible offence to the Hindu community. Yet their entire work consisted of aggressively manipulating the media on their clients' behalf, the same media that now rushed to lionize them.

During the ten years I lived in Los Angeles, I was struck by the number of professional people who chose to validate the worth of their business by emphasizing its links to the entertainment community. This went way beyond those restaurateurs who hang signed eight-by-ten glossy photographs of celebrities in their eateries; these were ordinary business people whose predisposition to the fame virus took the form of adding the words 'to the stars' after their profession. In my time there I met a realtor to the stars, a dentist to the stars, a personal fitness trainer to the stars (catchphrase: Body by Jake), an English-born veterinarian who called himself 'pet doctor to the stars' (his prominent clients included Doris Day), and of course, divorce lawyers to the stars and plastic surgeons to the stars. I met all these people through their personal publicists, who were employed specifically to raise their profile and make them celebrities. Spreading the word about their stellar client lists seemed the easiest means of enhancing their fame. Some 60 per cent of all Los Angeles physicians, according to one estimate in the early 1990s, had hired public relations firms.

Why did all these minor figures become celebrities of a sort? Partly because the media demanded it, but also because 'real' or traditional celebrities tended to play hard to get as soon as their fame peaked. They consented to interviews or television appearances only as and when it suited them, and that was often on a limited basis. Paul Newman is an example of someone who had become exactly as famous as he wanted to be by the early 1970s; he had no particular desire to seek more fame, and disliked the pandering to the media that would have been involved. Barbra Streisand likewise keeps herself loftily detached from media exposure. At their level, they can get away with it; no one in the Newman or Streisand entourage is likely to tell them to get out there and scare up some extra publicity. As for today's leading stars (Tom Cruise, Julia Roberts, Bruce Willis) the main role of their publicists is to turn down media requests for their time.

But their recalcitrance creates a vacuum, which is something the media abhor; hence the need for a more pliant, eager and available celebrity underclass to fill airtime and column inches. The proliferation of media in recent years has made necessary their unearned ascension to celebrity ranks. Even completely unknown people get a chance to give their dysfunctional personalities an airing on talk shows like Jerry Springer's. The net result has been to turn the viewing audience gradually into voyeurs, with dark needs that this long parade of preening exhibitionists exists to satisfy.

All the evidence suggests things will only get worse. The business of creating celebrities has reached a point of cynicism previously unattained, and the process by which fame is built up and then demolished has reached a dizzying speed. In 2001, a manufactured pop group named Hear'Say emerged, composed of five young wannabes who entered a TV contest on the programme *Popstars*, aimed at creating this group. There was nothing new in this concept; a wildly successful attempt in the 1960s had produced the Monkees. But remarkably, as soon as Hear'Say's five young members were announced, adverse or scandalous stories began appearing about them in the British press. Skeletons came tumbling out of closets, and old lovers began spreading scandal; the group were effectively being demolished before they were even strictly famous. Worse, some of the leaks about their errant behaviour appeared to emanate from the TV company that broadcast *Popstars*. During its run, the show's press officer Ian Johnson remarked: 'When the *Sun* demands six spreads in a week, I fear for my soul.' Everyone connected in the business of promoting these five young people appeared to have made the calculation that they were unlikely to figure in the public's consciousness for long, and could thus be treated as callously as the media desired.

Yet at least the members of Hear'Say were real, an attribute that no longer seems essential for becoming famous. In 1996, *Esquire* magazine conceived the notion of putting a fictional 'star' on its cover, along with a fulsome profile inside, as a subversive strike against celebrity culture. They chose a winning-looking young blonde woman, who was given the false name Allegra Coleman, and introduced her on its cover with the words: 'Forget Gwyneth [Paltrow], forget Mira [Sorvino] – here's Hollywood's next dream girl.' The article about her noted that directors Woody Allen and Bernardo Bertolucci, as well as New Age faith healer Deepak Chopra were ardent Allegra fans. It even detailed an 'on again, off again' romance she was supposedly having with the *Friends* actor David Schwimmer, and referred to scandalous nude photos of the couple frolicking on a beach.

Esquire's editor-in-chief termed the Allegra piece 'a brilliant parody of the brainless celebrity fluff that fills so much of the media these days'. Yet not everyone got the joke. Talent scouts at 20th Century-Fox pestered the magazine's offices until they were gently informed Allegra did not exist.

But of course the model who played Allegra did exist. Her name was Ali Larter, and she had made a couple of brief, undistinguished appearances on TV series. And wouldn't you know it, Allegra Coleman turned out to be her big break. She was immediately invited on to TV talk shows to discuss the *Esquire* hoax; and suddenly she had a movie career too. In 1999, she appeared in the films *Varsity Blues* and *Drive Me Crazy*, and has since gone on to appear in *Final Destination* and *Legally Blonde*.

Brad Follmer and Lauren Iungerich, two young entertainment industry staffers in Los Angeles, worked a comparable stunt. They dreamed up a fictional Scandinavian pop group called Skank, consisting of four implausibly attractive blonde models, and devised an entire history for them on a specially created website. (Wittily, they claimed Skank were winners of a music award called the Golden Olaf.) Follmer and Iungerich put together a product reel showing fake commercials featuring the girls of Skank, and sequences in which the girls modelled clothes on catwalks. At the Sundance Film Festival, which is heavily frequented by industry types looking for the next big thing, they put up flyers with the group's name and logo, and circulated a limited number of Skank ski-caps.

'We came across people there who talked to us and pretended to know about them,' Follmer told me. 'There were people talking knowledgeably about them, appropriating their name.' An article about Skank found its way into *Entertainment Weekly*; and the product reel led to Follmer and Iungerich becoming represented by the influential agency ICM. 'If you have something that seems fresh, hot, new and exciting, people will want it,' Follmer said. 'We were trying to wink at the audience, never to fool them. But some people just want to be fooled.' Quite so. If the Allegra Coleman and Skank stories have any moral, it may be that no parody of celebrity culture can be too broad to be taken at face value by people trained to sniff out commercial opportunities.

The logical progression, to create phoney celebrities who are not even real flesh and blood, has already happened. Lara Croft, the adventuress heroine of the Eidos video game *Tomb Raider*, is marketed like a real person, with her own history and what people in the movie business call a back story. The digital Lara Croft not only sells games, but appears on the cover of pop-culture magazines, and is used in commercials for the soft drink Lucozade. Ananova is billed as the world's first virtual newscaster, and can be seen on the Britain's Press Association website. T-babe is a cyber-pop star, a computer-generated model who has released a pop record. Oddly, their creators feel the need to give them biographies, and independent 'lives'. Ananova, who has hair with a greenish tinge and reads out news items in a mid-Atlantic accent, likes working out, skiing in the Alps and listening to Mozart; T-babe's creators reportedly spent a year giving her a psychological profile, with hobbies, parents, an ability to converse in four languages – and a pre-planned life story for her future.

The great virtue of cyberstars, of course, is that they will never tire of the pressures fame exerts on the most eager would-be celebrities of the human kind. One would have put Tanya Corrin in the 'most eager' category. Her boyfriend, an Internet entrepreneur named Josh Harris, asked her to join him in an experiment. He rigged up forty-two cameras in their New York loft that would record every second of the couple's lives for a hundred days; the results were to be seen on his website, WeLiveInPublic.com, which soon attracted a huge following. This went way beyond the *Big Brother* experiment; the all-seeing eyes were rigged up in their bathroom, their bedroom; and before long Tanya Corrin began to feel pursued. She began walking into the shower semi-clothed, and only stripping off inside, to hide her nakedness from the cameras. Visitors to the site could enter a chat room and comment on the proceedings, and a large number of them kept asking her to take her clothes off. Corrin finally snapped. The experiment ended on day seventy-eight, as did her relationship with Josh Harris. Writing about it in retrospect, she reported: 'The solitude is delicious. Privacy is sexy . . . it's a luxury I won't give up again so easily.'

It sounds like a cautionary tale. The Internet, of course, has become the medium of choice for non-celebrities to launch their bid for fame; who knows how many anonymous people have created their own websites, and faithfully record their thoughts, their opinions and the minutiae of their lives in the hope someone out there in cyberspace will find it fascinating? On occasions, one such anonymous person does this, and the trick works – they achieve fame of a kind. A young American woman named Jennifer Ringley has found a way to live a private life in public and apparently to do so with equanimity. Her website, Jennicam, which mainly shows her performing humdrum tasks in her Washington DC apartment, receives thousands of hits each day. She never turns the cameras off, not even when she is sleeping. Nor does she accede to the 150 or so requests from people logging that she take off her clothes for them. She can be seen without clothes, but only within the context of her life, so to speak.

Much of what can be seen on Jennicam is excruciatingly tedious, though it successfully holds the interest when compared to Jennifer's journal, a jotting of random daily thoughts unmediated by any obligation on her part to be entertaining. One such entry runs: 'On Friday, Dex drove an hour and a half south to pick up the RV [recreational vehicle] from his dad's place, then an hour and a half back north to pick me up from work early (hooray!), then 7 more hours up to Arcata. On Sunday we reversed the process, drove a straight 9 hours down to drop off the RV, then the hour and a half back home, where we arrived safe, tired, and covered in sweat and grime a little after 10.' And that was the day's highlight.

Jennifer Ringley has appeared on national television in America (including David Letterman's talk show) and it is hard to find a reason to reproach her. Whether she is lonely, bored, vain or starved for attention, she has found a legitimate way to validate herself in her own eyes. And since she charges for people to gaze on her mundane routine for hours on end, she is making money too. No, one cannot blame Jennifer, nor all the other minor would-be celebrities who feel entitled to their turn in the spotlight. Many of them may have a clear idea of their motives and aspirations. They are simply playing a game in which market forces offer them a chance of prominence. But even if they know what's in it for them, what's in it for the rest of us?

7
Playing at Fame

RULE SEVEN:
Some celebrities' entire public life is an act. They are playing themselves in their own movie

Let us take a famous person at random. Let us assume he is male. Let us study his demeanour as he appears in public – arriving at a glittering premiere or a political rally, being interviewed by the media, on the sofa next to a TV talk-show host. Can there be any doubt that even though he is not nominally acting, he is playing a role? What he is playing, in effect, is an idealized version of himself; he has found a way of presenting his best face to the audience. It is a form of low-key preening, and it has been learned by precedent. In recent years, a never-ending cast of celebrities has appeared in public; their every move has been caught by photographers or television cameras, and as a result, a certain mode of behaviour has evolved under such circumstances, and many of us have sub-consciously latched on to it. If hypothetically pressed into deputizing for a famous person in public, we would have a fair idea of the gestures and behaviour deemed appropriate.

Ordinary Americans, in particular, often seem extraordinarily at ease when a television reporter suddenly thrusts a microphone in their face and asks them to comment instantly on some topic. I am astonished by how many of them have absorbed enough TV etiquette to talk in a way that plays well on the small screen: plain, direct, but low-key, relaxed and never strident, in carefully modulated tones. These ordinary people give the impression of having waited their whole lives for this very moment, and having carefully rehearsed their lines. Of course, what they are exhibiting is learned behaviour, and Americans have had plenty of time to absorb the syntax of television, for no other nation in the world watches more of it.

But this may be unfair. A good many people the whole world over know how to behave when the spotlight and the cameras are turned upon them. Helen Fielding, the author of *Bridget Jones's Diary*, once took a TV crew to eastern Sudan to make a film for the British charity Comic Relief about the drought that plagues that barren land. At one point she and her crew came across a Beja tribesman called Mohammed Mahmoud, who spoke excellent English, and agreed to make a speech to camera about his people's plight. He was moving and eloquent: 'When he finished speaking, we were all tearfully overcome,' Fielding recalled. 'He then ruined the whole effect by turning to me, smirking, and saying "How did I do?"' But of course: playing at fame is a talent that can flourish anywhere.

Until recently, in Anaheim, southern California, in Disneyland's shadow, there was a bizarre tourist attraction called Tinseltown Studios. It was built to resemble a real Hollywood studio, complete with its own water tower, and at night searchlights scanned the skies above it. For $45, which included a three-course dinner, people could show up in evening dress and take part in a make-believe awards ceremony clearly modelled on the Oscars. At its entrance, they would sashay down a red carpet, while Tinseltown Studios employees in various guises sprang into action: as paparazzi, they brandished cameras and feverishly snapped the paying guests; as reporters, they shouted questions about their next movie; as teenage fans, they swooned and squealed at the sight of these celebrities-for-a-night; as waiters, they expressed weak-kneed admiration and coyly requested autographs. Inside, the guests were nominated for awards, and the winners got to make heartfelt acceptance speeches on stage.

As the promotional literature for Tinseltown Studios put it: '*You are the star!*' It was a means for Mr and Mrs Joe Public to luxuriate briefly in the stardust that eluded them in real life. But according to observers, the most disarming aspect of Tinseltown Studios was how convincingly the paying customers threw themselves into their roles; they smiled and waved confidently as they swaggered along the reception line; they were gracious but discreet with the 'reporters'; and some of their acceptance speeches perfectly captured the right tone, as heard on the Oscars or the Emmys. These folks had long been rehearsing in their minds for this stardom. They knew the drill, they knew the appropriate behaviour.

What is this behaviour? Let us go back to our random celebrity. On his arrival at a crowded event, he finds himself bathed in the glow of flash bulbs, and usually keeps moving (often from imperatives connected with security), striding purposefully towards his destination (the platform, the foyer of the theatre) but acknowledging the cheering crowd as he goes. The smile is broad, the wave expansive. Experienced operatives under these circumstances have perfected a stratagem that falsely suggests a familiarity with a fortunate individual while maintaining distance from the mass: a momentary acknowledgement of someone in the crowd by briefly pointing and waving at them, along with a complicated facial expression involving a fleeting smile, raised eyebrows and brief inclining of the head. By the time the crowd has craned its collective necks to see who has been picked out, the moment has passed and the celebrity has moved on. The first person I ever saw use this patently spurious device was President Ronald Reagan, an actor by profession, at a Republican political fund-raiser in Los Angeles. If Reagan imported this trick into the Presidential repertoire, it was Bill Clinton who perfected it, along with a virtuosic array of gestures involving real physical contact: hugs, two simultaneous one-handed clasps, even high fives, all executed while he is also moving along the greeting line impressively fast. George W. Bush does the point-wave-smile thing more often even than Clinton, but with less panache.

This little ruse, silly but harmless, is nevertheless emblematic of the built-in paradox that lies at the heart of the relationship between the famous and the non-famous. Its mixed underlying message may be summarized as embrace me, feel included in my glory, but keep your distance. The maddening, teasing, come-hither-stay-away dichotomy is also to be found in much of the body language exhibited by celebrities when they are under the gaze of cameras. I have always been struck by how much better famous people behave when they are on camera, as opposed to, say, being seated with a journalist bearing only a notebook and a tape recorder. In the latter situation, a faint air of petulance and a lack of grace may pervade the conversation: not quite enough to remark or report upon, but enough that it would make the celebrity look disagreeably supercilious through a camera's lens. We may assume, however, that this is closer to their 'authentic' behaviour.

In contrast, the behaviour exhibited for cameras, when the celebrity is being interviewed, or a talk-show guest, is beyond question an act, and also an extraordinarily complex construct. It often involves assuming a low-key, aw-shucks modesty, a gently teasing routine with the interviewer (maybe taking the form of a mild self-reflexive irritation with intrusive questions), and a reluctance to enter into areas of personal information, except in the form of previously rehearsed, though spontaneous-sounding statements. The more eminent the celebrity, the more practised they are likely to be in this area. The interview is a protracted negotiation in which the famous person must appear at all times a good sport, humorous and humble; he will often take the opportunity to express how lucky he feels to be the centre of attention on such occasions.

This, if you will, is the overarching behaviour, the facet of the act that reaches out to make an audience feel included and warm to the famous person. The underlying, distancing behaviour is harder to discern, but more often than not it is there too. It takes the form of an expression of amused disdain around the eyes, a conscious reining-in of laughter and other flamboyant responses. It is as if the famous person is consciously sending a series of messages to his brain that this is not the real him, that this is an act. Its almost subliminal delivery signals that only a few people close to him will have the privileged insight to look upon it and know it as an act. It is, in fact, a subtle means of asserting that the famous person would far rather not be in this position, playing to the rubes in the audience and evading crass lines of questioning; but it stops well short of making this distaste evident. It is a common shortcoming of the fan who is most overbearing and over-enthusiastic (and therefore most likely to be an object of contempt to the celebrity) that he will readily discern the more apparent, welcoming facet of the celebrity's behaviour, yet completely fail to read the underlying disdain. No wonder encounters between famous people and over-zealous fans are doomed to be brittle, even hostile exchanges, unsatisfactory to both sides.

The actor John Cusack once expressed to me his uneasiness about the odd balancing act of personae that is expected of TV talk-show guests: 'They want you to tell stories, and so you're encouraged to behave like a stand-up comic. But at the same time you're also making it clear that you're not. It's supposed to be you on that talk show, so you also have to perform being yourself. The whole process is weird. It makes me uneasy.'

Still, this playing at a version of oneself in public is a finite business; the walk along the red carpet to a premiere ends in the relative privacy of a theatre foyer, and even the most gruelling talk show reaches an eventual conclusion. But the problems become even more complex when the famous person is off duty but visibly trying to go about his own business in a public place; at this point, the disparity between his perceived public role and his private persona can seem huge and insurmountable.

Actors, especially, develop their own defences for walking around in public. Many will tell you there are two ways to walk down a city street – one way when it doesn't matter if you are recognized, while the second way virtually ensures you will not be recognized. It has to do less with disguises, and more to do with avoiding eye contact, the removal of swagger from one's walk, and a spatial awareness that involves keeping out of the path of others. Dustin Hoffman is one actor who is adept at this. I have twice passed him in crowded Manhattan streets, and he was playing it differently both times.

There are more calculating ways of melting into a crowd. David Bowie, who occasionally likes to travel on London Underground, says he favours 'wearing a hat and reading a Greek newspaper'. And then there is Woody Allen, who plays arguably the most complex game of all. Since he first became famous, he has consistently complained about ordinary people wanting to approach him and talk to him. Yet for all this, Allen behaves oddly, often walking through Manhattan in a series of heavy disguises (flat caps, raincoats tightly buttoned to the neck) so ludicrously ill-conceived that they only draw attention to his real identity. ('There goes Woody,' sigh jaded Manhattanites as he scurries past.) This is the polar opposite of hiding in plain sight. It says much about a man who so values his privacy that back in the 1970s, before I had even set foot in America, I knew Allen frequented an Upper East Side restaurant called Elaine's. I had only a sketchy idea of what the Upper East Side was: but from 3,000 miles away, I knew of this self-styled hermit's hangout. In a long line of falsely modest famous people before him (again, T. E. Lawrence comes to mind) Allen wants to be perceived as a man who backs only reluctantly into the limelight.

Still, one sees that it might be disconcerting to be approached by complete strangers who take for granted that they 'know' a famous person. What they are responding to is the way the famous person 'plays himself' in the public arena, at events that are pre-arranged, thus giving the time to rehearse his 'role'. Approaches by strangers are unscripted; they occur when the celebrity has stepped out of character and has reverted to being literally himself. On such occasions, the disparity between the private individual and the face he presents to the public becomes jarringly clear.

Far wider, of course, is the disparity between actors and the roles they play that enhance their fame. Relationships with the public are at their most blurred and uncertain among actors best known for playing one character.

Until 1999, Edie Falco was a jobbing New York actress, who worked mainly on stage. She was known and respected among a relatively limited industry crowd of fellow-actors, directors and casting directors. But then she landed a role on the TV series *The Sopranos*, playing Carmela, the big-haired, gaudily-dressed wife of New Jersey mobster Tony Soprano. At first she felt torn about taking the part: she had been appearing in a small theatre production, a play called *Side Man*, which began in an off-off-Broadway basement, and on the strength of terrific reviews and great word-of-mouth made it to Broadway. But Falco was cheated out of her Broadway debut, because she had filmed one episode of *The Sopranos*; to her surprise the cable TV channel HBO liked it enough to commission thirteen more, and she was contracted to make them.

Within weeks, her life became an entirely different proposition. 'For seven years, I had been living in a teensy studio apartment, a fifth floor walk-up with no kitchen,' she said. 'My first thought was, I'll make enough money now to move, which was a very big deal. So I bought a stunning loft overlooking the West River. I felt quite adult.'

Falco told me this in London, where she was appearing in a short run of *Side Man* in the West End; in Britain, *The Sopranos* is nowhere near the cultural event it became in America, and she was relieved to be somewhere she was not widely recognized. In person, she dresses quite unlike Carmela Soprano – casual, basic black, and no big hair, long fingernails, jewellery or rhinestone sweaters. 'What changed everything with *The Sopranos* for me was the attention,' she reflected. 'I've spent a lot of years as an actress being able to live anonymously in Manhattan. It's a lovely life if you work occasionally. Then along comes what Tom Hanks calls this white-hot attention. It really got a little out of hand. It happened hugely and quickly. I had gotten comfortable with my place in the industry. People who knew of me liked my work, and I felt, you can't ask for much more than that, really.

'Now with all this, the accolades, the gowns, the awards, I look in the mirror and wonder, what became of the life I'd known fifteen years previously? All I wished for was not to have to do another job outside acting to support myself. But all this other stuff – I didn't bank on it, I wasn't prepared for it, and I'm not entirely sure I'm enjoying it. I walk down the street and people say, "ahhh, I see your disguise". It's odd, the things people feel free to say to you once you're on their TV. You're public property.

'I've often woken up in the morning, thinking I was still me, then I remember the circumstance of my life being so different, and I almost work myself up into an anxiety attack about it. I used to spend days walking around the city, living my little life, watching other people. That's changed. Now when I watch them they've been watching me first. Landing at Heathrow, walking around London, I'm not recognized as much. I feel like myself again, the Edie I knew for many years. I had no idea it would affect me the way it does. Being de Niro or Woody Allen, what must that be like?

'I've walked on stage in New York and people applauded as if it was Carmela. Women rush up to me in the streets and scream "Carmela, we want you to come to our pyjama party!" At some level it's flattering, on another it's terrifying. I'm trying to find a comfortable place to exist within it.'

Those women have simply fallen victim to the fame virus: they see a TV star on the street, and become disproportionately excited. For Edie Falco fame has proved a difficult transition. The sudden attention has dealt a blow to her sense of identity; she feels like public property, she is wondering what became of her life, and feels a loss of 'the Edie I knew for many years'. Such disadvantages go with the territory, and she needs to find a way to balance them with the positive benefits her fame has brought her.

At least Carmela Soprano is a fictional character, and Falco has no responsibility to her role beyond playing it to the best of her ability. When actors play real people, their relationship with an appreciative public can be even more entangled. In 1993, Liam Neeson starred in Steven Spielberg's film *Schindler's List* as Oskar Schindler, a real-life German Catholic war profiteer who was moved to save 1,100 Polish Jews from certain death in Nazi concentration camps by employing them in his factory. Neeson's towering performance in the film was rewarded with an Oscar nomination.

Shortly after the film's release, Neeson told me, he was walking in Manhattan when an elderly Jewish man approached him: 'I stopped, out of deference to his age. He had tears in his eyes. He shook my hand and said: "Thank you for saving my people." I walked on a bit, and then I thought I couldn't let this go. I was sure this man had gone through something horrible in his life. So I ran back to him and tried to explain: "I'm an actor. I'm only forty years old. I couldn't have lived through what your family lived through. I appreciate your sentiments, but please bear in mind, I'm only an actor."'

After this incident, Neeson said, he began to contemplate the influence film stars wield: 'It's one thing if you're playing Batman. But doing *Schindler's List* made me aware of the importance of what you say on a thirty-foot screen that twenty million people are going to see. I'm not saying I want to play good guys all the time from now on. But it's made me wary about doing some piece-of-trash film just because it's got a big budget.'

Also in *Schindler's List* was Ben Kingsley, who while making the film experienced an uglier side of human behaviour stemming from a confusion between acting and reality. While the cast and crew were shooting, in and around the city of Cracow, Poland, passers-by would occasionally shout anti-Semitic insults. And in the hotel where they all stayed, Kingsley and a handful of actors were sitting at the bar drinking one evening when an elderly man approached one of them and asked if he was Jewish. The actor replied that he was, and the old man drew a finger across his throat, then pulled his fist up behind his neck, indicating a noose. Kingsley leaped at the man, and a scuffle ensued.

Twenty years on, Kingsley is still best known for playing a real man who did good deeds, Mahatma Gandhi. His title role in the 1982 film won him an Oscar, and he then found himself playing saintly, if isolated and lonely real-life characters for years: the Talmudic scholar Itzhak Stern in *Schindler's List* and Nazi-hunter Simon Wiesenthal, as well as the prophet Moses for a TV movie. The assumption widely held by strangers who meet Kingsley is that he is somehow rather saintly himself, a notion he finds distressing: 'I know I act as a way of getting from A to Z,' he said. 'It's a vehicle to get to where I want to be as a human being. I certainly don't think I was there when I won the Academy Award for Gandhi. Everyone thought I was. Everyone was convinced that [in playing the role] I spiritually evolved. But I didn't spiritually evolve. I worked my socks off. I learned my lines, lost a lot of weight [twenty pounds], acquired the most eccentric set of mannerisms ever seen on a screen, and an accent that I researched. I didn't have time to spiritually evolve. And you don't spiritually evolve by playing spiritual men. It doesn't rub off. It's a paradox, but it's true. The evolving, the growing as a person, comes out of the effort of working.'

Yet Falco, Neeson and Kingsley are all actors, and though they have encountered varying degrees of difficulty in reconciling their real lives with the roles they play, they are at least free to move from role to role. Yet there is another class of famous person, the uber-celebrity, whose entire life in public appears to be an act. They are playing themselves in what amounts to their own movie: the world, if you will, is their soundstage. There was something of this in Muhammad Ali in his prime. The same is true of the deeply odd, unknowable Michael Jackson – as a boy an exuberant young African-American, who evolved into what now looks like a light-skinned, troubled-looking female catwalk model.

Then there is Madonna, the doyenne of recent uber-celebrities. She re-invents herself continually, seeming to don and doff masks, identities and worldviews with the changing of each season; the thought has often occurred whether there are areas of her life in which cameras could not intrude. Her ex-lover Warren Beatty, a man with long experience of being a figure in the public eye, seemed to find himself drawn involuntarily into Madonna's web of fame management more subtly than he knew: theirs was an event relationship, conducted during the making of his film *Dick Tracy*, in which she co-starred. But as soon as it opened to mediocre business, the couple were history.

One might easily dismiss Madonna as a fame addict, but she told me a different story. When we met, in her large secluded house perched on top of Mulholland Canyon in Los Angeles, she was about to sell her second home in New York City because of the relentless intrusion. It's an odd paradox that many famous people find it hard to conduct their lives in supposedly sophisticated New York without passers-by and paparazzi gawping and taking pictures, whereas in Los Angeles, a city with attitudes that are strikingly more provincial, the famous can move around easily. 'The attitude to celebrities in LA is, there's so many of them, no one really cares,' Madonna said. 'Which is fine by me. People tend to leave you alone here.

'I don't feel like being chased by paparazzi, and every time I walk out of my house in New York, they're there. And if you're in New York, you're in the newspapers every day, no matter what you do or don't do. I can be in the New York papers every other day even when I'm not there. I constantly read that I've been seen in a restaurant or shopping and I wasn't there.'

I commented that she sounded almost exhausted by her fame. 'It's not "almost", I'm exhausted with it now,' she said. 'Fame? I wouldn't wish it on my worst enemy's dog. You don't realize what horrible entrapment fame is until it's too late. And you can tell that to everyone in the world who says they want to be famous, and they won't listen to you. They don't want to hear that, because it's safer for them to imagine that people who are famous or celebrities are the happiest, most privileged people in the world. And if you destroy that concept for them, then they might just possibly have to view us as human beings. And that would be all too much.' She laughed, rather mirthlessly. So even all her material gains were not worth it? 'No.' Could she imagine a parallel adult life in which she was never famous, but just an average person? 'I don't know what an average person is.'

Given all this, it was no real surprise when Madonna moved to London – partly to be near her boyfriend Guy Ritchie, whom she later married, and partly because the environment for celebrities is relatively relaxed. The British are as fascinated to read and gossip about famous people as any nationality on earth, but if they confront them on the streets, they display a certain reticence. And although London boasts a tabloid press that is the most competitive on earth, and among the most vicious, its paparazzi lack tenacity; they are less likely to maintain a watching vigil outside Madonna's home than their Manhattan counterparts. It's a city that seems to suit her. The degree of attention she receives is muted and civilized, but it never falls below a level where she might begin to miss it.

Any discussion about Madonna swiftly turns to her fame and her own relationship to it. It is a subject that she keeps firmly on her own agenda, and her constant re-inventions are conducted with one eye on how they will be received by the public and media. She appears to be playing at fame, while at the same time watching herself doing it. One might argue that this is the inevitable lot of today's uber-celebrities, but not so long ago, it did not have to be that way.

For six or seven years, the Beatles were more famous than Madonna has ever been, and the amount of attention they received and intrusiveness they suffered was far greater. Yet it must be said that they handled their fame with a charm and grace that seems beyond the grasp of many famous people of the present day.

They had advantages, of course, in the form of each other. It must surely be easier to deflect the attacks on one's sense of self that arrive in the wake of mass adulation when one has three friends around for company, all of whom have gone through precisely the same journey from obscurity to world renown. From the outset, the Beatles were adept at sharing out their fame equally, doling out their sardonic wit together at press conferences, deflecting question after question around the four of them so that each mop-top was included. Interestingly, no one Beatle ever emerged as the fans' overwhelming favourite, even though John Lennon and Paul McCartney were clearly functioning as the group's creative engine. Instead, the Beatles operated like four facets of one likeable, talented, amusing young man – the rebel, the quiet one, the clown and the cute one.

Set beside the celebrities of the new century, the Beatles come across as relatively unspoiled and spontaneous. It wasn't quite true, of course. Their manager Brian Epstein had knocked off some of their rougher edges, had sacked their original drummer Pete Best to make way for the nominally more appealing Ringo Starr, and ordered them to wear identical suits on stage. In this superficial sense, they were a manufactured group.

But crucially, they were not manufactured people. Each of them had an unforced brashness, a zest for life and a strong sense of authenticity. In public, they said what they meant. Intelligent, fast-talking and adept at thinking on their feet, the Beatles had no need to play at fame. They could simply be themselves, and with no apparent calculation still achieve greater fame than any other people on earth in the 1960s. No matter how celebrated they became, they each essentially presented something close to their real selves to the public, and they never fell back on sounding bland or falsely conciliatory. Only rarely did they do or say anything that could be considered a PR gaffe. John Lennon's (correct) assertion that the Beatles were more popular than Christ backfired when it enraged America's fundamentalist right; while the ill-fated trip to India to sit at the feet of the Maharishi Mahesh Yogi soon looked like a mistake. But typically, it was a mistake that at least three of the Beatles admitted: Lennon even wrote a cheekily subversive song, 'Sexy Sadie', about the guru. I have met McCartney and Starr, and both men, given their history and their fame, are remarkably natural and free of pretension.

Artistically, the growth of the group corresponded with all four of them asserting themselves as individuals. The problem wasn't that the entire Beatles phenomenon was phoney or inauthentic, but simply that four opinionated, strong-minded men found it hard to maintain the fiction that each was primarily part of a unit. As solo artists, McCartney and Lennon suddenly seemed poles apart; and it came as a surprise to no one that the period shortly after the Beatles finally broke up coincided with a brief flowering of George Harrison's long-suppressed songwriting talents.

After John Lennon's assassination, the surviving trio could have paraded their fame ostentatiously by appearing in public with phalanxes of security men. They refused to do it. 'I had a couple of bodyguards with me for a few weeks,' Starr said. 'But they soon went. You can't go on living in fear. And you know, President Reagan got shot. If the President can't be properly protected, what chance do other people have?'

I once interviewed McCartney in a suite at the Beverly Hills Hotel, where he told me: 'There's security here right now. I couldn't tell you exactly where they are, but I believe this room is being made secure by someone, so I have faith that the best security around will do its job. One of my requests is that they do it invisibly, which is what the best security's about, anyway. I do it, I take care of it and forget it. I wouldn't want to live with the constant oppression of a little army of SAS men around.' On this trip to America, McCartney jogged in public each morning; in New York, he jogged in Central Park, a hundred yards from where Lennon was gunned down. In London he still occasionally travels by Tube; people stare at him, but assume that if this is the Tube, that cannot really be Paul McCartney.

He claimed a particular relationship with people when he is in public, which keeps them friendly but at a distance: 'I don't know what it is. People tend not to bother me too much. Whether it's because I've made appeals for privacy, whether they understand that it would bug me, I don't know. I mean, I go out to the pictures, and I don't go in disguise. If I've promised the kids I'll take them, that overrides the feeling that no way could I go out in the street because I'd be mobbed.'

Or it may just be that as adults, after they broke up as a group, the feeling the Beatles inspired in their fans was an amiable, proportionate affection. The Sunday in 2001 after George Harrison died, I was having lunch with friends in St John's Wood, north London; after the meal, someone suggested that we stroll down to Abbey Road studios, one of the world's foremost Beatle shrines, and see what was going on. Dozens of people had gathered on the pavement in front of the studio railings, and the usual paraphernalia of fandom was in evidence: imploring messages conveying a sense of personal loss were pinned on the fence, and candles were left burning on its low wall, as if to some saint in a Catholic church. But in complete contrast to the excessive, media-fuelled outpourings of grief over the death of Princess Diana, no one at Abbey Road was hysterical or overwrought, just a little melancholy. Complete strangers nodded, smiled, chatted, and exchanged memories of the Fab Four. The scene was not even devoid of humour. Some fan had left a message with the scrawl: 'Say hi to Elvis!' One imagined Harrison would have laughed at that.

This may be largely a personal bias, since I went through my teenage years idolizing them, but the Beatles seem to me to have exhibited as much grace and charm under pressure as any truly famous people in recent years. (Given what the world put them through, this is no mean achievement; remember that apart from Lennon's tragic death, George Harrison was also the victim of an assassination attempt.) They were phenomenally skilled at dictating the terms and limits of their fame, rather than allowing that fame dictate to them and affect their public personae. Even now, in advanced middle age, the two survivors seem unspoiled and natural.

This is not to say they are completely artless in their dealings with their public. When I met McCartney, he was extraordinarily attentive, asking about my British roots, how I had come to find work in America, flatteringly making the odd joke that could only be shared by two English men. It was a dazzling performance; for the ninety minutes I was with him, he made me feel at the centre of his world. Even while I understood I was being manipulated, I was lulled into feeling he and I had a unique understanding of each other; he remains the only famous person who ever elicited such feelings.

A few years later, I was with the late Derek Taylor, for many years the Beatles' press officer at Apple. Unprompted by me, the subject of McCartney came up, and Taylor began to talk about his knack of focusing on the person he is with, turning those big mournful eyes of his on them, and making them feel that, very sincerely, they are the most important person in his life. 'And ten minutes later, when their back's turned,' Taylor said, laughing, 'he'll be off doing it to someone else.' I said nothing, but such is the Beatles' allure, I could not even bring myself to feel irritation at McCartney's wiles. Even now, given how wearing it must be on the psyche for someone like him constantly to meet people on such unequal terms of familiarity, I think he handled himself well. Was he playing at fame? Just a little, perhaps.

8
Involuntary Fame

RULE EIGHT:
Once fame enters your life, whether you invite it in or not, it's hard to live down

Striving for fame is not an essential component of attaining it; there are occasions when it simply descends on individuals, through no fault or effort of their own. One can be born into celebrity; Prince Charles is an example of someone who appears to find his fame inevitable (because of the dynasty he was born into) but irritating (because the media slavishly follow him wherever he goes and faithfully report his every throwaway comment). One can arrive in the world medically unique, like Canada's remarkable Dionne sisters, the first known quintuplets to survive infancy, or Louise Brown, the world's first test-tube baby. One can be given a work assignment that makes you world-famous; it happened to Neil Armstrong, the first man to walk on the moon. Or one can simply find oneself in a particularly telling time and place in history entering a photographer's viewfinder; think of that pitiful, naked young Vietnamese girl, running down a road, crying in anguish from her napalm burns. She had no say in the matter, but her picture played its part in shifting neutral opinion against the Vietnam War.

Sometimes a single snapshot encapsulates an historic moment in a way mere words cannot. One recalls the image of Jacqueline Kennedy clambering over the back seat of the presidential convertible in the Dallas motorcade, desperately trying to get help for her mortally wounded husband. A few days later came another picture with indelible power: the Kennedys' three-year-old son John-John bravely saluting his father's coffin in a silently eloquent summation of America's grief. Jacqueline Kennedy and her son were already world-famous: those photographs sealed for them an immortality they had not sought.

In America in 1974, there was only one picture that counted, and it was both vivid and stunningly surprising. It is not even a photograph as such, but a single frame of film shot on a surveillance camera. It shows a dark-haired young woman brandishing a carbine, in the act of holding up a San Francisco bank.

In this iconic picture, she looks the very embodiment of radical chic – thin as a rail, with a beret on top of her shaggy shoulder-length hair. While hers is the stance and manner of a desperate young subversive, there is also an intriguingly plaintive look in her eyes. The picture made the cover of *Time* magazine, and for a spell its subject, Patty Hearst, became the world's most famous young woman. To this day she is one of the great examples of involuntary fame; she neither asked for it nor expected it. Patty was an unlikely revolutionary, to put it mildly. She was an heiress born into a conservative publishing dynasty; William Randolph Hearst, the flamboyant, super-rich newspaper baron on whom Orson Welles based his film *Citizen Kane*, was her grandfather.

At the age of nineteen, her life was proceeding uneventfully and predictably. As a college student at Berkeley, she became engaged to a respectable young man named Steven Weed. Patty had some interest in art, and thought she might eventually land a job at a museum, or maybe work for an art magazine like *Connoisseur*. She had no reason to expect much beyond taking her place in San Francisco's young high-society set and living an affluent, comfortable life.

Her plans were changed drastically when she was kidnapped by an obscure radical group, the Symbionese Liberation Army, and held captive in a small San Francisco studio apartment for fifty-seven days. The SLA gave her a codename – Tania – that soon became familiar to the whole world. She joined them in a series of robberies, including the fateful one captured on the surveillance camera. Finally she was captured by police, and served twenty-one months in prison before President Carter commuted her sentence, allowing her release into her parents' custody.

She maintained from the outset that she had been brainwashed and raped by SLA members, who had coerced her into joining their criminal activities. But in 1974 America was a very different country, one in which paranoia was rampant and conspiracy theories plentiful. Almost immediately after the disclosure that Patty Hearst was joining in the SLA's crime sprees, rumours sprung up that she had organized her own kidnapping, that her marijuana supplier at Berkeley was an SLA member, and that far from being an unwilling participant, Hearst had sympathized with the SLA's beliefs and methods.

Meeting Hearst now, those conspiracy theories seem far-fetched. She has essentially reverted to type and insists on being called Patricia rather than Patty. She lives in some style in a large Connecticut home, and has the manner of a society matron; her two teenage daughters have made an appearance in New York debutante circles. It is easy now to accept her insistence that she felt she had no option but to participate in the SLA's criminal activities, and psychologists at the time claimed that she was a victim of 'Stockholm Syndrome'. (Interestingly, this phrase, which describes a hostage's emotional attachment to captors arising from stress, dependency and a need to co-operate for survival, was coined only the year before Hearst's kidnap; in 1973, a Swedish bank teller became romantically involved with a robber who held her hostage.)

But the single most intriguing facet of Hearst's subsequent life, given that fame crashed in on her against her will, has been her relationship to that fame. Many of us, having survived the traumatic circumstances that led to such a brush with worldwide fame, might desire a life far removed from public attention.

Initially, this seemed to be her strategy. She married Bernard Shaw, a quietly-spoken former San Francisco policeman who became her bodyguard after she was released from jail. But then she decided to write an autobiography, *Every Secret Thing*, which detailed the SLA affair from her point of view. She agreed to sell the film rights of the book to a Hollywood producer named Marvin Worth. And when the film, *Patty Hearst*, was finally completed (with Natasha Richardson in the title role) she accepted an invitation to attend its premiere at the Cannes Film Festival.

'It seemed a bit much,' Hearst told me ironically, in her languid voice. 'But I thought I'd like to go. Why not? It would probably be the only time I'd attend anything like this.'

At a dinner party in Cannes before the picture was screened, she met the American film director John Waters, famous for making bad-taste, low-budget camp classics like *Pink Flamingos* which included a scene featuring his friend, the male transvestite Divine, eating dog faeces.

Given the horrors she had experienced at the hands of the SLA, Hearst might easily have given Waters a wide berth. It transpires that he harboured an obsession with Hearst, and kept a shrine to her in the bathroom of his Baltimore home. A visiting reporter has described it as 'lovingly displayed', and noted that it included 'the actual glasses she was wearing when she was arrested'.

So did Hearst run for the hills when Waters told her he wanted her to appear in one of his films? She did not. Instead, she let it be known that she found the suggestion agreeable. Thus began one of the most irredeemably minor acting careers in movie history. In *Cry Baby* (1990) she played the mother of a character played by Traci Lords, best known as a former under-age porn actress. In *Serial Mom* (1994), Hearst took the role of Juror No. 8. In a rare departure from Waters's films, she again played a mother in a teen comedy, *Bio-Dome*, described by critic Leonard Maltin as 'a bomb' characterized by 'crude writing and inept plotting'. In 1998 Hearst returned to the Waters fold with a cameo role in *Pecker*.

But her most astonishing appearance was her cameo in Waters's *Cecil B. Demented* (2000). It wasn't the role itself – yet again, she was playing someone's mom – but the film's storyline. The title character is a deranged guerrilla film director who despises mainstream movies. He and his renegade gang of teenage revolutionaries kidnap an A-list Hollywood actress (Melanie Griffith) and force her to star in their underground film. Sounds familiar, doesn't it?

Hearst was completely aware of the parallels with her life in *Cecil B. Demented*. 'I told [Waters] I really should sue him for copyright infringement,' she recalled. 'He said: "It's not about you, but there are similarities." I told him he had a lot of nerve. We had a good time shooting it, though at one point he said to me: "I'm glad your mother is not alive to see this. I'm feeling really guilty right now."'

Since then, she has launched herself into a fledgling career as a TV presenter, starting off by presenting a cable documentary about the history of Hearst Castle, her grandfather's palatial California home.

Why did she do all this? Certainly not for the money. She claims she genuinely likes the work, and it helps distance her from her past: 'I'd like to do more of it. My kids say to me, "We wish you weren't gone." But my stock answer to them is, it's the only time I'm truly happy – if only to teach them you have to do something productive, and you should love what you do. For me, it's been an effort for my own sanity not to be a victim. That's been hard. I love acting and I love presenting. I'm lucky to be able to work in the film industry and I want to keep doing it. I've had to struggle to make sure I can make a life beyond one horrible event, and for that to be it. You just have to fight to make a life the way you want it.'

Yet there may be more to it. Hearst first experienced fame under desperately unpleasant circumstances. But with the distancing effect of time, she has come to find the condition of celebrity itself rather agreeable. She can even reprise aspects of her former life, only without the unpleasant bits, while remaining a focus of public attention. Once she was a kidnapped celebrity; now she appears in a wry, satirical film about one.

I talked to her at length about all this at a convention of television critics at a luxury hotel in Pasadena, California. She appeared at a press conference to promote her documentary about Hearst Castle, spoke with me for a couple of hours, then left with her husband in a limousine. A velvet rope had been placed at the entrance to the hotel, on a long walkway between the door and the kerb, for photographers wishing to take pictures of arriving and departing celebrities to stand behind. More than a few of these photographers looked distinctly non-professional – the sort of sad amateurs who combined taking pictures with pleading for autographs – but Hearst took one look at them and instantly went into star mode, preening and sashaying before them, turning her hips, tossing her hair, posing at their every whim. She looked in her element, at the centre of their attentions. After the terrible things that happened to her in 1974, Patricia Hearst might seem an odd candidate to succumb to the fame virus. But she definitely tests positive.

I know of no other person who has set himself so squarely against fame and its trappings as Charles Webb has done. If his name sounds only dimly familiar, that means he's been doing his job properly.

In 1962, on a writing fellowship at the age of twenty-three, he wrote his first book. It was published the following year to reasonable, if muted acclaim. 'It got good reviews,' said Webb. 'It didn't sell fantastically, but it did OK for a first novel.'

Titled *The Graduate*, it was about an alienated young man named Benjamin Braddock, who obtains a degree from a small college, flies home, insists to his affluent parents that he has no career plans, and begs to be left alone. He resents the fact that they view his academic achievements in status terms. He slouches around the house, drinking beer, watching TV and floating in the pool. He embarks on a joyless affair with a formidable older woman, Mrs Robinson, the scheming alcoholic wife of his father's business partner. Then he falls in love with Elaine, Mrs Robinson's daughter. And the vengeful Mrs Robinson sets out to ruin him.

In 1963, the film producer Lawrence Turman bought the movie rights and hired Mike Nichols, then a hot stage name, to direct. Dustin Hoffman, an unknown off-Broadway actor who had never set foot on a film set, was cast as Benjamin; he was thirty years old, playing twenty-one. Anne Bancroft, cast as the 'older woman' Mrs Robinson, was actually only five years older than Hoffman.

On the face of it, all the elements were slightly off-kilter, but on its release in the 'summer of love' in 1967 *The Graduate* became one of the biggest movie hits of the decade. Benjamin Braddock was an ideal anti-hero for a generation of American youth disaffected by the Vietnam War and disillusioned about their future. The film also got seven Oscar nominations, and Nichols picked up an Academy Award. Simon and Garfunkel's chirpy incidental score, especially the song 'Mrs Robinson', became a classic.

Everyone, in fact, enjoyed career advancement from *The Graduate* – except for its originator, Charles Webb. He was and is an anti-materialist, and the book was semi-autobiographical; a doctor's son, he grew up in an affluent, privileged Los Angeles suburb, attended prep school, then an Ivy League college in Massachusetts. There he met, fell in love with and married Eve Rudd, a similarly bohemian young woman from a rich background, who became the inspiration for Elaine Robinson.

Until the mid-1970s he wrote eight or nine more novels (none of which achieved a fraction of the sales or acclaim of his first), and then abruptly stopped. Meanwhile, Eve pursued a career as a feminist artist.

From the outset they rejected materialism, fame and all its trappings; Webb donated the royalties from *The Graduate* to a civil liberties organization. They eked out a spartan existence, taking low-paid jobs, and often not working at all. At one point they lived in a French nudist community. I first met them in what was then their home, a modest trailer park in Ojai, California, in 1982. Neither was working; she had dropped her surname in the cause of gender politics, and insisted on being known by the single first name Fred. They had removed their two teenage sons from school and were educating them at home. It looked like poverty-level existence.

'We ran out of money completely a couple of times,' Webb told me years later. 'It's a purifying experience. There's nothing like it. It focuses the mind like nothing else, makes you see things you can't under any other circumstances. You sometimes regret you're not the kind of person who has sorted out insurance policies and savings bonds. But you reach a certain point where you have flashes of insight into things. It's high-wire stuff.'

Webb not only feels *The Graduate* has been a millstone around his neck, he even regards being constantly tagged as its author as a form of discrimination. 'The stereotype of the creative person is something I've come to feel I understand at this point. I run up against the phrase "author of *The Graduate*" everywhere I turn, whether in publishing a book, finding a place to live or going for a bite at a cafe. Like any other stereotype it carries with it a frustration, because it's a discriminatory factor in one's life.'

If this seems stubborn self-denial, Webb at least practises it in his life. 'The last time we ran right out of money, we went into a series of menial jobs. We worked in an inn in Connecticut. I washed dishes, and Fred made sandwiches in the kitchen. No one knew who we were at first, but then our cover was blown, and one of the chefs asked Fred if he could have my autograph. I told her to tell him no. But he wouldn't accept that. So finally, I told him I'd give him my autograph if he'd give me his. He wouldn't do it. Not only that, but he was offended by the suggestion.'

One often wonders about the motives of autograph hunters. Is their tenacity born of a desire to sell a celebrity autograph to the highest bidder? But in that case, why did the chef react so strongly to the idea of giving Webb his own signature? Maybe because it inverts what we think of as fame's natural order. Webb's proposition involved a disassembling of dreams, a democratization of the hierarchy of celebrity, one that would assign an obscure chef and a semi-famous author equal 'importance'. It was too much for the poor man to handle.

Webb's career has an ironic coda. He and Fred decided to leave the United States in 1999 and settled in Britain, moving into a draughty, almost unfurnished flat in an unlovely south coast town. They exiled themselves because they could no longer stand the materialism of America, and because Webb was also weary of being pigeonholed in the US as the man who wrote *The Graduate*. In America, each of his successive novels was simply deemed inferior; in Britain, where all his books were respectfully reviewed, he felt he might finally be free of the association.

He saw my byline in a British newspaper and contacted me; I was the only person in Britain whose name he knew. We arranged to meet, and I was able to tell him something that dismayed him – that *The Graduate*, having been a successful novel and a hugely popular movie, had now been adapted for the stage and was due to open in London's West End. Webb was mortified: 'We come to Britain to escape from *The Graduate*, and this happens,' he complained. 'It's like it follows us around.' He had no idea the story was going to be staged.

But then, why would he know? He had given up any financial rights to the hydra-headed beast some thirty-five years earlier. When the production opened in 2000, Webb, on infrequent trips to London, would wander past the Shaftesbury Avenue theatre where it was playing. He would gaze up at the enormous marquee advertising, and managed to find some comfort in his long-standing decision to turn his back on fame and money. 'I think if I'd still had a financial interest in the thing, I'd find it pretty disgusting,' he said. 'I'm glad I have nothing to do with it any more. So I'm free to just feel amused about it all.'

What do the stories of Patty Hearst and Charles Webb tell us of the nature of fame? Certainly this much: once it enters your life, whether you invite it or not, it is a hard thing to live down. In Hearst's case, it arrived under unwelcome circumstances, but however repelled she may have felt by the SLA trauma, that defining event of her life has left her with a complex and ambivalent attitude towards her own celebrity. She may talk about it in ironic, flippant terms, but it still appears to exercise its spell. As for Webb, he was pleased that his first novel got published, and content that it was positively reviewed. But it did not occur to him that fame would ensue; in 1962, writers whose works were published did not automatically speculate about the chances of selling the movie rights. Still, though Webb has energetically attempted to brush off the trappings of fame, it is something from which he has never quite managed to escape. Being perceived as the man who wrote *The Graduate* makes him angry and upset to this day.

At least Hearst and Webb have found a way to live functional lives in the wake of fame's uninvited arrival. In contrast, the story of Canada's Dionne quintuplets is perhaps the most melancholy example of the havoc involuntary fame can wreak on innocent lives.

The five identical girls – Annette, Emilie, Yvonne, Cecile and Marie – were born two months prematurely to an impoverished French-Canadian farmer and his wife in rural Ontario in 1934. They each weighed less than two pounds, and their survival was miraculous; in fact they were the first quintuplets known to survive infancy. The media learned of their birth only after their father called a local newspaper to ask if a birth announcement for five babies would cost the same as for one. This tells us much about his innocence of fame's machinations; but in fairness to him, the most cynical sophisticates could scarcely have imagined subsequent events.

The quintuplets swiftly became global celebrities, and were the sensations of Depression-era Canada. The doctor who delivered them, Allan Roy Dafoe, became a celebrity in his own right. The five girls were taken away from their parents and became wards of the Ontario Government, under Dafoe's supervision. They were placed in a home across the road from their parents' house, which the state turned into a theme park and named Quintland. The girls were put on display behind a one-way glass screen, and three times a day up to 6,000 visitors filed through Quintland to gawk at these curiosities at play.

It was a freak show, but one with enormous commercial potential. Dr Dafoe took it on himself to organize advertising deals for the quintuplets, and their images appeared on hundreds of products, ranging from corn syrup to breakfast cereal. They were a money machine, and it didn't stop there; a whole new Dionne business sprang up in North Bay, the nearest sizeable town, and suddenly thousands of unemployed residents had jobs. Sales of Dionne dolls outstripped even those of Shirley Temple. Even Hollywood got into the act, with three movies about them (*The Country Doctor*, *Five of a Kind* and *Reunion*) between 1936 and 1938, as well as a Disney cartoon, *Pluto's Quin-Puplets*. All this happened half a century before people started using the word 'commodification', but the Dionne quintuplets were commodities above all else.

If anything, things got worse. Their father successfully petitioned courts to regain custody of his daughters, and they returned home at the age of nine. But in 1995 the three surviving sisters (Emilie had died aged twenty and Marie aged thirty-six) claimed their father had sexually abused all five of them for years; he would take them out one at a time in the family car to assault them. Annette Dionne claimed she tried to discuss the abuse with a Roman Catholic priest who shrugged aside her complaint, suggesting the girls wore thick coats on their car rides.

As adults, the three surviving sisters became increasingly open in their criticisms of the Catholic Church and the state of Ontario. They eventually filed a $10 million suit against the state Government, claiming they were wrongly deprived of a share of the earnings from tourism. In 1998 they were awarded $4 million compensation.

They eloquently expressed their feelings about the treatment they had received in a sympathetic open letter to the parents of the McCaughey septuplets, born in Iowa in 1997. 'Our lives have been ruined by the exploitation we suffered at the hands of the Government of Ontario, our place of birth,' they wrote. 'We hope your children receive more respect than we did. Their fate should be no different from that of other children. Multiple births should not be confused with entertainment, nor should they be an opportunity to sell products.'

But of course the Dionne quintuplets had no way of knowing their existence was part of a huge business bandwagon, and everyone involved in it had a vested interest in keeping it rolling – the doctor, the priests, the ad agencies, the Hollywood executives, the sponsors of products they endorsed – and the state of Ontario, which viewed their arrival as a small economic miracle in a time of hardship. It is doubtful that anyone would have stepped in to halt the Dionne bonanza, even if the unpalatable facts of their story were made known.

The Dionnes had the bad luck to remain unique, and therefore objects of curiosity, throughout their formative years. If they had been born fifty years later, the growing number of multiple births facilitated by fertility drugs would have helped return them to relative obscurity. Louise Brown, the world's first test-tube baby, was born in Bristol in 1978, and initially she was a good media story: 'a truck driver's miracle child', as the Associated Press greeted her birth. The day she took her first faltering steps was duly recorded, as was her first day at school. But she never had to suffer the crass exploitation endured by the Dionnes, and in any case the frequency of subsequent in vitro fertilizations (50,000 over the next twenty years in the United States alone) removed the impetus for intrusive publicity.

The Dionnes' story illustrates a harsh fact about involuntary fame: you may find yourself subjected to it, but if it continues to grow beyond a certain point, it takes on a life of its own independent of you, and you no longer have much power to control or modify it.

While this is true of Hearst and the Dionnes, who can justifiably be viewed as innocent victims of fame, it is equally true of people who initially embraced fame but have subsequently come to find it distasteful; they quickly learn that fame makes no distinctions regarding their approval of the process. I have already discussed the brilliant mathematician and disabled genius Stephen Hawking, who set out to make theoretical physics accessible to the masses, wrote an international best-seller and made himself the best-known scientist since Einstein. Hawking has since been the subject of lurid, unwelcome media reporting of his marriage break up and his personal life.

He is by no means alone. The pages of tabloid newspapers are filled with people who contentedly allowed themselves to become famous for a particular gift, but later became infamous for less laudable attributes. Once, Mike Tyson was known primarily as the most fearsome heavyweight boxer for a generation; but now he is as famous for sexual assaults on young women as for being the world champ. Each time any of these women lodges a complaint against Tyson, his name makes headlines all over again.

For many years, the Manchester United footballer George Best was idolized as one of the world's greatest wingers, a reputation that remained unsullied by his well-reported weakness for attractive blonde women. But since the end of his playing career Best's alcoholism has been the main story, and each time he succumbs and takes a drink in a public place the media inevitably report the fact in sensationalist terms.

Sean Penn was once known as one of America's most gifted, intense young screen actors. Then in 1985 he married Madonna, one of the most famous and photographed women in the world. Almost overnight Penn's role became relegated to that of Mr Madonna. And then another reputation overtook him, that of a man who would happily lash out at photographers who harassed or annoyed him; he served thirty-two days in jail for assaulting an extra who tried to take his photo on the set of the film *Colours*.

This unhappy new image came to haunt him. In 1991 I met his second wife Robin Wright on the set of a small Irish film, *The Playboys*. Penn accompanied her to Ireland, but stayed out of sight in their hotel room. One day I met an Irish tabloid photographer hanging about outside the hotel, and asked who he was waiting for. When he told me it was Penn, I naïvely replied I didn't think he had plans to meet the press. 'Ah, but you see,' said the photographer, 'if he comes out and I can persuade him to have a pop at me, give me a whack, that's a front-page picture.' Time after time, Penn fell into this transparent trap. I relayed the Irish story to him years later, and he closed his eyes tight and shook his head in disgust. Despite his tough-talking, bad-boy image, he seemed unable to imagine anyone picking a fight with him for such calculating reasons.

In a similar category to Penn is his friend Robert Downey Jr., also feted as a brilliant young actor when he first emerged in the 1980s. Downey had first used hard drugs when still in his teens, but would turn his angelic, innocent gaze on anyone who asked about his wild days and swear he had put them behind him. I first met him while he was making *Chaplin*, the 1992 film that won him an Oscar nomination in the title role. One location used for the film was Park Plaza, an old building near downtown Los Angeles; in the 1980s it had been the venue for a club called Power Tools, popular with a rich, hedonistic young crowd who enjoyed a sex-and-drugs lifestyle. Downey recalled with amusement that he had been an habitué. 'The year 1985 was a blur in these lobbies,' Downey told me. 'I look back on it, and it's so passé. When you're in the middle of all that, drugs are it. Then you look back on it all, and it's laughable. It seems like for me that's all really over.'

Fat chance. Downey has been living his life in denial ever since, and has consistently failed to kick his drug habit. Violating his parole conditions for drug offences has landed him in jail and lost him acting work; he is now far more famous for his addictions than for the talent that made him a celebrity in the first instance.

At least Downey got to enjoy the initial advantages of fame, the upside, before his enslavement to drugs became the only story about him. Other people who went out of their way to distance themselves from their fame found it a tough proposition. Greta Garbo is an obvious case in point. Between 1926 and 1939 she enjoyed a stellar career in movies, and even made the difficult transition from silent pictures to talkies – a good trick, given her exotic Scandinavian accent. A prickly, elusive character, she never wanted to deal with the studios' publicity divisions, preferring to let her luminous screen presence do the talking. Confronted by the press about her affair with actor John Gilbert, she stayed maddeningly silent.

Abruptly she quit her career in 1941, aged thirty-six, never deigning to explain why, although the reviews for her final film, *Two-Faced Woman*, probably contributed to the decision. She became a recluse, dividing her time between Manhattan and Switzerland, and for the most part her strategy worked. But she failed to appreciate that in the absence of any other story about her, her very reclusiveness became the story. She acquired rarity value; for several years before her death in 1990, photographic evidence of a Garbo sighting was quite literally a prize. And sadly, the more dishevelled and sickly she looked, the greater the sums the paparazzi could charge for their snatched shots. It was a cruel finale to her life, one that she had done nothing to deserve.

A handful of literary figures have adopted the Garbo philosophy towards fame. Cormac McCarthy, author of the novel *All the Pretty Horses*, does nothing to co-operate with his publishers' desires to publicize him, and has effectively kept a low profile. So has J. D. Salinger, lionized in the 1950s for *Catcher in the Rye* and *Franny and Zooey*. Yet Salinger's enduring reputation has made it hard for him to maintain his privacy; like Garbo, his reclusiveness is the story. It is a melancholy fact that the best-known photograph of Salinger shows him open-mouthed in horror at the realization that he is being photographed against his will. He even fought a long, bitter lawsuit to prevent the author Ian Hamilton from using his letters in a biography. Hamilton, whose *In Search of J. D. Salinger* details his attempts to track the great man down, appeared to regard Salinger's stated desire for peace and privacy as a marketing device that he needed to outwit in order to get his book written.

There is no clear moral to be drawn from Salinger's story, or Garbo's, or that of anyone else who becomes an involuntary victim of fame. Given that fame is an amorphous entity, with no tangible characteristics, no emotions, and certainly no value system, it is hard to fight off. You may want no part of fame. But that doesn't mean you don't have to deal with it.

9

Flourishing with Fame

RULE NINE:
People who handle fame well tend to be those with talents or genuine achievements

It's unquestionably true that fame can distort, disorient, and on occasions even destroy people to whom it happens. In discussing it, most famous people choose to concentrate on the negative aspects it has introduced into their lives. Yet there are those for whom fame seems tailor-made. They feel gratitude for having attained it; it even seems to complete them as personalities. They may be in a minority, but some people undoubtedly flourish in celebrity's unrelenting glare.

One would have to travel widely to meet a more enthusiastic advocate for the consequences of fame than Dolly Parton. When I asked her if celebrity had been 100 per cent beneficial in her life, her reply was swift and unequivocal: 'It's not kept me 100 per cent happy, or meant that I haven't suffered greatly. But I've never ever thought I made a mistake, going into this business, or that maybe I should get out of this business. For every price I've had to pay for celebrity, like not being able to do certain things, I think of all the great things I've got to do because of it.

'So what if I can't go shopping in the middle of the day? I can have them open up the shop early. I wouldn't trade it, and yes, it's been more than I could ever imagine. My life is more than most lives are. When you're starting out, you just hope to do well, make a good living, maybe buy a car, then a second car, a place at the lake, money to travel. But my life has been so blessed, I would be an idiot and a fool and an ungrateful bitch ever to complain about the few bad things that come along.

'It amazes me when I hear some celebrities, and I count many of them as friends, talking about it. I think, "What is your problem? You are so ungrateful." They hate their fans. They don't want anything to do with this or that. I hear these stories that you're not allowed to look a certain star in the eye on a film set, shit like that. I think, "What is your problem? You should be so thankful, on your knees, thanking God that you ain't having to work for a living. You ain't having to do something you don't want to do."'

To put Parton's enthusiasm into context, it helps to know something of her origins. She grew up one of twelve children in the Smoky Mountains of east Tennessee. At the time she was born, in 1946, her house had no electricity, and the roads to it were unpaved. The Parton house was not tiny, but nevertheless its fourteen family members had to share four bedrooms. She now makes jokes about how poor she used to be ('We had running water. We had to run outside to get it!'). All this is part of her amiable country-girl *shtick*, but it does not detract from the grinding poverty she knew growing up. Her father Lee did several jobs to make ends meet. He farmed tobacco, worked on construction jobs in Knoxville, the nearest sizeable city, and when the family's potato crop needed harvesting, he would keep his children home from school to help him dig them up.

One of Parton's earliest hits was a song she wrote herself, 'Coat of Many Colours', and it reflected an incident that actually happened to her as a nine-year-old. There was not enough money to buy a new coat for her first school photograph, so her mother Avie Lee fashioned one from variously coloured scraps of cloth, and told Dolly the Bible story of Joseph and his coat of many colours while she made it. When Dolly arrived at school in this ragged garb, her classmates taunted her, broke some buttons off the coat and pushed her inside a dark clothes closet.

Parton's upbringing has left an indelible mark on her, one that informs her attitude to her fame. She says now of her career as an entertainer and singer: 'It's better than hauling corn or planting tobacco. I've been there. I remember, I always wanted to be a star, and I try to remember never to complain about the fact that I am. I have my problems, but I'd have those same problems no matter what business I was in. I think there are fewer problems because I'm in control, I have the money to go and do something else, or I can kick the door in and have it replaced if I get that mad, which I don't. I can rant and rave and still be thankful for my job. So it's been more than I deserve or ever expected, and I wouldn't take nothing in place of it.'

Now the head of a substantial business empire, she has a fortune estimated at over $100 million. Parton runs the Dollywood theme park near where she grew up, a tourist attraction that draws two million visitors annually. She has launched a dinner-theatre chain called Dixie Stampede in four US cities. And at the age of nineteen, when she was just starting out as a singer, she made a decision to retain all the rights to her songwriting and publishing, and stuck to it – sometimes at considerable cost.

In the early 1970s Elvis Presley wanted to record Parton's song 'I Will Always Love You', but the request came with a condition: Presley always took half the publishing royalties for any song he recorded. Parton turned him down, but was distressed because she badly wanted Presley to sing her song. A stalemate ensued and it never happened. Two decades later Whitney Houston revived the song for the soundtrack of the film *The Bodyguard*, and the record became one of the top-selling singles of the 1990s. Before the song even dropped out of the charts, Parton was $6 million richer, and jubilant that she did not need to give half her new fortune to Presley's estate.

This had nothing to do with personal avarice. Parton, who is childless, is the *de facto* head of her extended family, and has made it her destiny as a famous and wealthy woman to take care of their needs. 'People ask, why are you still working?' she mused. 'And I say, because I have a family to feed. Every day I get up and feel I have to go to work. There are new ones coming along all the time. I'm from a family of twelve (one brother died as an infant), and they all have big families. I'm the only one who's making any money to speak of. They're wonderful people, but if there's a crippled child or one that's sick, I have to be there. I'll pay for the kids' dental work, and I'll get them a new car if they graduate high school. The way I look at it is, they're my family and I'm very close to them. I can't give them all they want, but I can give them all they need. They look to me.'

When the squabble with Presley occurred, she says she told his representatives: 'The song's published, it belongs in my house, and this is what I'm going to feed my brothers and sisters and nephews and nieces with. I cannot give up half.'

She has some thirty nephews and nieces, a growing number of grand nephews and nieces, as well as a network of uncles, aunts and cousins.

She presides over a clan of about a hundred people. 'There's a great need. Do you think I'm going to stand around, let someone go sick or need something?'

Beyond doubt, Parton's fame has been a redemptive force in her life. She has gone out of her way to embrace it, happily donning extravagant wigs and flashy outfits, and openly discussing her pneumatic body shape and the efforts of her plastic surgeons, all the while playing on her outrageous persona with teasing humour and charm. She has found a way to handle celebrity on her terms, and finds its disadvantages trifling compared to the benefits of caring for her huge family. 'It gives me a reason to live and work,' she said. 'It gives me depth and soul and heart. I need to be needed.'

Fame in America can be redemptive for those who grow up in poor circumstances. Ray Charles and Stevie Wonder are two artists who were born into poverty, and faced the extra handicap of permanent blindness. The conversations of both men are peppered with expressions of gratitude for their fame. 'Never once did I imagine I would be here,' Wonder told me. 'It didn't have to be this way.' It certainly didn't; both he and Charles were at least born into a time when their music crossed cultural boundaries and made them international stars; too many of their predecessors, generations of hugely talented Afro-American blues and r-and-b musicians, started out poor and obscure, and died in the same circumstances – their work often having been stolen by a white-controlled music industry.

The influential talk-show host and actress Oprah Winfrey was born in Mississippi to unwed parents, who separated and sent her to be raised by her grandmother on a farm with no indoor plumbing. Even in such an unpromising environment, she seemed a remarkable child; at the age of three she was reading the Bible and reciting in church. Precociously, she asked her kindergarten teacher to advance her to the first grade; and then she skipped second grade.

She moved to Milwaukee to live with her mother when she was six. From the age of nine, as she has revealed as an adult, she was abused sexually by male family members and their acquaintances. Only when she was fourteen did her abilities begin to flower; she moved to Nashville to live with her father, who instilled in her a daunting work ethic.

Winfrey became a part-time radio announcer at seventeen, and worked her way through various jobs in news radio and television before taking over an ailing local TV talk show, *AM Chicago*, and making it so successful that it was nationally syndicated. Renamed *The Oprah Winfrey Show*, it became one of the most popular programmes in TV history. She now presides over her own business empire, Harpo Inc. (so called because it is her first name spelled backwards) and is personally worth half a billion dollars.

Winfrey is another example of someone who employs her fame positively, while never forgetting her early circumstances. In 1994 President Clinton signed legislation designed to protect children from abuse; so hard had Winfrey lobbied for it that it became universally known as the Oprah Bill. Acknowledging the importance of literacy, and recalling the prodigious reading ability that first got her noticed as a child, she started the Oprah Book Club, so astoundingly influential that any book she chose to feature immediately became a best-seller in the US. On her show she began 'the world's largest piggy bank', inviting viewers to send in small change. Their donations totalled $1 million; Winfrey matched it, then used the accumulated sum to launch a scheme to send disadvantaged students to college. Her aims are hardly modest: through her show, she wants her (mainly female) viewers to improve their lives, and thus improve the world.

Public interest in Winfrey's life has been almost obsessive, befitting someone once described in *Vanity Fair* as having more influence on the culture than any politician or university professor, and second only to that of the Pope. She has divulged her problems with cocaine; details of her often alarmingly fluctuating weight have filled news columns over the years. Yet she has managed to manipulate her own fame, and make it work for her in pursuance of several social agendas in which she feels personally vested.

Like Parton and Winfrey, Billy Bob Thornton, the actor, director and screenwriter, was raised poor in the south, in a small Arkansas town. Fame for him has been a great social equalizer; when he first moved to Los Angeles, and tried to explain his ideas for films to sceptical Hollywood executives, he recalls encountering almost open derision.

'It shifts your psychology around a lot,' he said of the celebrity status he enjoys now. 'Certain aspects can be brought out in you that were dormant. Initially, it gave me the confidence that I lacked. Being well-received gave me the confidence to keep doing what I was doing. It made me feel less of the stigma I grew up with, being from the south and therefore stupid. People used to hear my accent and make assumptions. Fame probably helped my work in some ways, because I would probably take more chances creatively.

'In other ways it hasn't changed me at all. I probably have the same pants I had when I was eighteen. I wear expensive clothing – vintage T-shirts, these boots I'm wearing are expensive. Certain restaurants look at you funny, but I've always had an aversion to suits.'

On a personal level, Thornton has found that widespread public approval, exemplified by the actor Robert Duvall dubbing him 'the hillbilly Orson Welles', has filled a gap in his life. 'I appreciated it so much, the way he meant it. I don't know how to react to compliments sometimes. If someone says they like something I did, I'm thrilled like a schoolchild. I've spent my entire life trying to get my father's approval, which I didn't get from him. So I seek the approval of people like Robert Duvall. If he feels that comment of his is accurate, well, that's enough.'

For some people, fame becomes a means of resolving parental issues or conflicts from childhood. Critics have argued that Steven Spielberg, whose parents divorced when he was a child, has used his stellar directing career as a means of re-creating the idyllic boyhood life he knew before they separated. (Some critics also carp consistently about Spielberg's need as an adult to be in touch with his 'inner child'.) This slightly crude argument has a subtler variant: that much of his creative output is linked more or less directly to seeking his father's approval. It is a proposition Spielberg himself does not quite deny.

During the Second World War, Arnold Spielberg served in Burma, as a radio operator on B-25s. This fact impressed his young son enormously, and a high percentage of his films – the *Indiana Jones* trilogy, *Empire of the Sun*, *1941*, *Schindler's List*, *Saving Private Ryan* and the epic TV series *Band of Brothers* – are set in that period.

'It goes even further back for me,' Spielberg told me. 'Because my father had fought in World War II, my first movies that I made when I was twelve or thirteen years old were 8 mm. movies about that war. *Escape to Nowhere* was about Americans fighting Germans in North

Africa. My second was forty-five minutes long, black and white, no sound, 8 mm., called *Fighter Squadron*. And that was about World War II pilots. I went out to this airport, Sky Harbor in Phoenix, Arizona, which in the late '50s and early '60s still had World War II airplanes sitting on the tarmac. And they let me get into them with my twelve- and thirteen-year-old friends, pretend we were flying them and film it all. So I can honestly say I've been making WW II movies all my life. I've been stuck in the '40s most of my career.'

If Spielberg's fame has given him carte blanche through his films to lay to rest some of the darker times of his childhood, it has also allowed him to exercise a deeply felt sense of social responsibility. He is known as one of Hollywood's richest men, having directed some of the highest grossing films in history – *Jaws, E.T., Indiana Jones, Jurassic Park*. From *Jurassic Park* alone he is said to have pocketed $294 million. But philanthropy, mostly practised anonymously, plays a major part in his life.

'It was my mom and dad who taught me the gift of giving,' he told me. 'When I was making those 8 mm. movies in Arizona between the ages of twelve and sixteen, I donated most of the proceeds from them to the Perry Institute for mentally handicapped children. I learned this in temple. I learned about the pride you get and feel inside, that you can only give yourself by giving to someone who's not a member of the family, but a stranger.

'That's something I knew all my life. My parents were philanthropic without really having the money to be philanthropic. So I've always given my mom and dad credit for breeding that into me. It was something I knew how to do without ever being taught how. It was just something that went along with being a member of our family.

'I've read things that say people like me are philanthropic just to generate publicity for themselves. This rampant cynicism about philanthropy is disgusting. I don't put my name on most of the stuff I give away. Also, in Judaism God doesn't acknowledge named gifts, only anonymous gifts. It's not acknowledged by the temple, nor by *shuls* all over the world. It doesn't count if your name's on it. That's in the Talmud.'

His last reference is significant. Around the time of making

Schindler's List, about a German industrialist who saved more than a thousand Jews from Nazi death camps, Spielberg went through a period of authentic moral growth. He seriously began to embrace his Jewishness, an identity he had brushed aside in his adult life up to that point. His second wife Kate Capshaw converted to Judaism, and they decided to raise their children (including their two adopted children of Afro-American descent) as Jews.

And he began finding ways to give away huge portions of his vast wealth. With the profits from *Schindler's List*, which he felt disinclined to keep, calling it blood money, he started the Righteous Persons Foundation, a body that dispenses funds to Holocaust and Jewish continuity projects. He was also moved to launch the Survivors of the Shoah Visual History Foundation, a huge video archive of more than 50,000 Holocaust survivors telling their life stories to camera. Their testimony is used as a teaching aid in schools; it is also carefully indexed and transmitted via fibre-optic cables to Holocaust museums and archives throughout the world. And, in a neat detail that brings this story full circle, Spielberg appointed his father Arnold chief consultant of the Foundation's fibre-optic network. There is no question that fifteen years of fame, and a reputation in Hollywood for churning out film after hugely successful film, finally liberated Spielberg to the extent of launching these initiatives – a process that began when he insisted on making *Schindler's List*.

When I met him in Cracow, southern Poland, in 1993, when the film was being shot, he told me: 'I couldn't have made this film until this point in my life. I needed to get my head out of a viewfinder, live life a little.' Fame (and, of course, great wealth) enables one to do just that; after *Schindler's List*, Spielberg also concentrated far harder on becoming a father and family man. It would be four more years before he would embark on directing another film.

Using one's fame to pursue a social agenda can effect some kind of personal transformation. As a pop singer, Dublin-born Bob Geldof of the Boomtown Rats was successful if hardly memorable. But his Damascus Road moment came when in 1984, at the age of thirty, he watched a BBC television documentary about famine in Ethiopia, flew to Africa to observe the situation for himself, then returned to London and self-consciously used his own celebrity to gather a collection of pop stars to record a charity single under the name Band Aid. The song, 'Do They Know It's Christmas?', became the biggest-selling single in Britain, and inspired a similar charity record in the US, 'We Are The World'. The following year Geldof helped organize Live Aid, an international charity event involving two simultaneous concerts in London and Philadelphia. The proceeds and other donations raised millions of dollars to feed starving Africans.

Geldof, now widely known as 'Saint Bob' in the tabloid press, was knighted by the Queen and nominated for the Nobel Peace Prize. His autobiography, *Is That It?*, became a best-seller. The fact that the Boomtown Rats disbanded in 1986 merited only a brief news item; he had re-invented himself, redeemed himself through his own fame.

That isn't to say the subsequent years have been kind to Geldof. He went through a wrenching divorce from his wife Paula Yates, with whom he had been involved for fourteen years; ironically, he indirectly helped it to happen. He set up an independent television company, Planet 24, which produced an irreverent morning talk show called *The Big Breakfast*. Yates was featured, interviewing celebrity guests on a bed; one of them was Michael Hutchence, the singer with Australian rock group INXS, for whom Yates left Geldof. (Later, Hutchence hanged himself and Yates died after an overdose of pills.)

Despite all this, Geldof remains a more substantial man than he was before Live Aid. He still makes records, and has a diversity of business interests. But his fame has given him a moral stature, and he still uses it to further his geo-political interests; most recently he has been vocal in various political forums attempting to persuade Western nations to forgive the crippling debts of Third World countries.

Shirley Temple's defining moment came even earlier in her life. She was, of course, the most popular child star in history, and had made twenty films by the time she was six years old. The leading box office draw in the US in the 1930s, her cheerful radiance helped Americans through the Depression. President Roosevelt, praising her 'infectious optimism', extravagantly declared: 'As long as our country has Shirley Temple, we will be all right.'

Temple peaked at the age of twelve, having made forty-four films. In her teens she made a few more, though she never managed to kindle the same spark. She wed in her teens, but the relationship ended swiftly.

When she was twenty-one and newly divorced, she decided to take the first holiday of her life, and visited Hawaii. There she met Charles Black, who became her second husband. From then on she never made another film, and decided to dedicate her life to public service as a supporter of the Republican Party. She served four US presidents. Richard Nixon appointed her US representative to the UN in 1969. Under Gerald Ford she was ambassador to Ghana, and later the first woman to become White House chief of protocol. In the Reagan administration she was a foreign affairs officer in the State Department; George Bush appointed her ambassador to Czechoslovakia. It goes without saying that wherever she went, people remembered her primarily as the chirpy little tot from the 1930s movies.

Many people at the time found Temple's act too wholesome and saccharine for words, and predictable child-star stories surfaced about her: a pushy mother, a grasping studio inflicting a punishing work routine, cheerful smiles that masked childish heartbreak. But she consistently denied it all, profusely thanking her mother in her autobiography, and insisting she would not have changed a minute of her life. Still, the fact that she escaped from Hollywood is a telling one; and the rich, rather distinguished life she enjoyed afterwards suggests she finally found the means to use her celebrity in a way she found satisfying.

There are rare people, neither born in poverty nor undergoing any apparent transformation, who simply embrace fame with apparently effortless ease, slipping into it like a pair of comfortable old shoes, and proceeding through life as if their fame were the most natural condition in the world. Mick Jagger comes into this category. He has been famous for literally his entire adult life: the Rolling Stones became a nationally known group in Britain in 1963, shortly before he turned twenty. Since then he has remained one of the most internationally recognized figures in popular culture. Jagger donned the mantle of fame with the ease of one accepting a long-awaited inheritance, and set about modifying the unspoken rules of behaviour expected of stars. He was not the first celebrity to partake of illegal drugs, but what set him apart from predecessors was his casual refusal to deny that he used them. Nor did he propagate the myth that he held much of a brief for monogamy. Jagger knew instinctively that the Stones' initial appeal was as avatars of youthful rebellion, and he played up to this image with a kind of amused disdain.

The paradox about such a radical, even revolutionary icon as Jagger was that fame enabled him to indulge his patrician tastes. He seemed an untamed rebel, but in fact he was a clever boy who had grown up in a comfortable middle-class family. He even loved cricket, for goodness sake. Fame broadened his horizons considerably, and eventually he gravitated to a circle of minor British aristocrats within his age group, with whom he felt instinctively at ease. He soon revealed himself as an international jetsetter with a weakness for large properties dotted around the globe.

Even more remarkably, this scourge of polite society proved to be an adept capitalist. Jagger, along with his hand-picked advisers, used his fame to invent a profitable new model for rock tours. 'There wasn't a role model, a money model or business model for making money as a performer in pop music,' he told me, 'not without playing Vegas or having your own TV show. And they weren't attractive, they obviously wouldn't be much fun. You could see they hadn't done Elvis Presley any good.

'So the new model, touring arenas, was invented at the end of the '60s, and it's still the bread and butter of what tours are. The Rolling Stones 1969 tour was the first like that. You had your own sound, your own lights, an uncluttered stage. You could make money like that without it being too expensive [for fans] to go to.

'Before that, on tour, you never knew where you were going to be – you could be in a tiny barn with your own speakers, or a large theatre. You never knew what the size of your stage was. This was like inventing your own staging, your own space. You were doing your show, and you weren't being imposed upon. We had our own people, but before then there was no industry, so we had to take people out of other fields – *Holiday on Ice* and things like that, people who knew good sound and lights. Until then there was no workforce for touring.'

Having made this radical innovation in pop performance, Jagger spent years ruthlessly refining the business model to a corporate sheen. Rolling Stones tours are now marathon affairs, often lasting two years and spanning the globe; they employ hundreds of people, a travelling company of experts who ensure a continuity and uniformity of standard. A Stones concert will be as impeccably prepared and executed in Bangkok as in Boston.

It is as if Jagger has always taken his fame for granted, knows his worth and status precisely, and refuses to be constricted by the traditions of the entertainment industry in advancing his business and career ideas. Certainly he stays aloof from the by-products of fame; it is hard to think of an occasion when he has betrayed signs of vulnerability when confronted by its excesses. He can look weary or impatient when the media intrude on him, and he admitted to me his irritation at its inaccuracy. Presumably he is not overjoyed at the zealous reporting of his dalliances with mostly younger women. Yet he never lashes out or loses his temper publicly; he retains his peculiar sense of *noblesse oblige* – or maybe genuine disdain. Nor is Jagger a man who will confess publicly to personal problems or moments of despair; indeed, one imagines he would find it vulgar to do so. Instead he is a skilled practitioner of evasion in his dealings with his fans and with the press; he was once accurately described in the magazine *Musician* as 'the rock star who doesn't love you, doesn't need you and doesn't lie about it'.

However, he does admit that celebrity has coloured his existence. He conceded to me that so much of his life has been lived in the shadow of fame that it would be hard for him to imagine life without it.

'I'd have to go back to when I was quite young to remember [not being famous]. Of course it must have had an effect on me. You really have to fight against it, so you try to be as grounded as possible in your life. But you can forget sometimes, and then maybe people who don't know you very well will say something. Someone said to me recently at the airport, "You spend an awful lot of time trying to avoid people!" Well, no, it's just that you have a certain way of living that you have that you don't question. And all this came about just so I didn't have to spend another half hour in an airport lounge.' He grinned slyly. 'Most people would love not to do that. So sometimes you get brought up a little bit by those things. Someone says that, and you think, oh, do I? So yes, you're slightly cut off, maybe. But so what? I'm not missing anything that much.

'You can try and overcompensate for it by, say, standing in overcrowded, not very nice pubs. And where does that get you? Nowhere.

You're just stuck in the public bar of the Chiswick Arms. Then you say to your mates, "I went to the Chiswick Arms." Another grin. "Well, so-fucking-what? It's difficult to be natural about all this. It's about play-acting. I try to be as normal as possible, but I think it does affect things around you. But you've just got to laugh. I take it with a sense of humour.'

So one can experience fame without coming to harm; indeed, it can come to seem like an opportunity to be grasped. But it is notable that the people who seem to flourish in experiencing it tend to be people with talents and genuine achievements. Jagger and Parton are undeniably gifted musicians, who share a head for business. Thornton is an accomplished screenwriter; Winfrey would surely have been a successful entrepreneur, whatever field she had chosen. None of them is defined by fame; the bulk of what they actually do is well away from the public gaze. One cannot imagine any of them sitting around idly waiting for the phone to ring, or dashing to an event simply because it offers media exposure or a photo opportunity. These people are all self-starters, each with an agenda of their own. Their celebrity, when it came along, only enhanced the remarkable assets they already possessed.

10

The Pitfalls of Fame

RULE TEN:
Despite the allure of fame, it barely registers as a factor in determining quality of life

The distinguished American psychologist Mihaly Csikszentmihalyi has spent years studying 'optimal experiences', those times when people report feelings of deep contentment in their lives. He has concluded that what makes life profoundly satisfying is a state of consciousness he calls 'flow'. It is not easy to define; indeed, Csikszentmihalyi observes that it differs from person to person, and that many individuals reach a state of flow by trial and error. But he makes a brave stab at definition: 'The best moments usually occur when a person's body or mind is stretched to its limits in a voluntary effort to accomplish something difficult and worthwhile.'

'In the long run,' he adds, 'optimal experiences add up to a sense of mastery – or perhaps better, a sense of participation in determining the content of life – that comes as close to what is usually meant by happiness as anything else we can conceivably imagine.'

Professor Csikszentmihalyi, formerly chairman of the Department of Psychology at the University of Chicago, assembled a research team and asked them and colleagues across the world to interview thousands of people from different walks of life. They found that the description of the flow experience was essentially the same, irrespective of age, gender, cultural differences, affluence or poverty.

The professor, then, is one of the great experts on the subject of human happiness. But here is an apparent paradox: despite the fact that vast numbers of people long to achieve fame because they believe it will enrich their lives, it is a subject virtually absent from his researches and his books, *Flow* and *Living Well*.

Of course, it is no paradox at all. Despite its allure, attained fame barely registers as a factor in determining quality of life. And when

THE PITFALLS OF FAME

one surveys those lives that have encountered fame, the spectacle is not exactly edifying. The incidence of divorces, alcoholism, drug abuse, suicide achieved and attempted, deprived, unhappy or dysfunctional childhoods is acknowledged to be greater among the famous than the obscure. Even when we subtract what we might call the headline-grabbing items from the list of fame's disadvantages, it can still feel like something disappointing and anti-climactic, quite unrelated to Csikszentmihalyi's optimal experiences.

In her autobiography *Learning To Fly*, Victoria Beckham of the Spice Girls records that as a child she wanted to be famous because fame would stop her feeling empty inside. (Though she has never said so specifically, one can almost guarantee it has not worked.) The British soul singer Lisa Stansfield wistfully and unknowingly put her finger on a major problem with fame: 'I thought some magic, sparkly thing would happen to me, and it never did.'

The key phrase there is 'happen to'. Stansfield couches fame in passive terms, as something external that might, on arriving in her life, have the power to make her feel better; it requires no active role on her part. This notion is diametrically opposed to Csikszentmihalyi's formulation that optimal experiences add up to 'a sense of participation in determining the content of life'.

Things do happen to famous people, of course, but many of them are not particularly welcome. One of the most common is the degree to which self-absorption becomes a dominant feature of their personality, to the extent that it is almost a cliché. The American TV producer Roger Director, author of a satirical novel about the TV industry called *A Place To Fall*, says of his book's protagonist, an overnight celebrity: 'There's nothing particularly original about the character of an actor who was swabbing a bar top one day, then becomes a star and lets it go to his head and turns into a jerk. It's part of the Hollywood story. You can pick up any issue of *People* magazine and see four or five possible people like this ... That kind of behaviour's repeated year in and year out, over and over. Weird people enter this business, and it certainly exerts a lot of emotional torque.'

It does, and examples of monstrously egotistical behaviour abound. The phrase 'Do you know who I am?' yelled angrily by celebrities at recalcitrant maître d's and doormen, is so commonplace to have become clichéd. It has been reported that the actor Val Kilmer has in the past instructed extras, crew members and other underlings on their films not to make direct eye contact with him. Yes, Val Kilmer.

One reason Roger Director's words carry weight is that he worked on the hit TV series *Moonlighting*, a comedy drama about a pair of private eyes, starring Cybill Shepherd and Bruce Willis. At the outset, Shepherd was an established Hollywood name, while Willis was an unknown actor who literally was swabbing bar tops in New York City immediately before he was hired. Yet Willis's character David Addison – fast-talking, funny, with a perpetual sly grin – was arguably the more attractive role. Shepherd was known to be a demanding personality, but no one could have predicted that putting her and Willis together would cause quite such a combustible clash of egos. The pair seemed to loathe each other on sight, and their continuing feuds caused production on *Moonlighting* to close down more than once. And essentially all they were doing in these unseemly squabbles was asserting their own importance over the other – fighting for fame.

Willis, of course, went on to become a major movie star, but was still prone to outbursts that suggested he alone knew the true worth of his talents, while the rest of the world was simply out of step. At a Cannes Film Festival press conference held to publicize *Armageddon*, the 1998 film in which he starred, he responded to mild objections about the movie from film critics with the curious assertion that few people read the printed word any more, and that their objections were thus unimportant.

Willis may have said a few preposterous things over the years, but he has never indulged in a flamboyant parade of his wealth to the same extent as the pop singer Elton John. It's not merely that John has a fortune thought to be close to £200 million; it is his profligacy at spending it that raises eyebrows. A glimpse of this trait emerged during his 2001 claim in the High Court against his former manager and financial advisers; in one twenty-month period, he was said to have spent almost £40 million. This included £9.6 million on property and, in many ways even more astoundingly, £293,000 on flowers. (At one point, the singer had two florists on his personal payroll.) Asked in court how this was possible, he replied, with no apparent trace of irony: 'I like flowers.'

THE PITFALLS OF FAME

Elton John's life has certainly not been marked by unblemished contentment; in his time he has fallen prey to cocaine and alcohol addiction. Those close to him maintain he has a complex and often sceptical attitude towards his own fame. Yet if that is true, he sometimes has a peculiar way of demonstrating it. He is prone to public tantrums; even a documentary made about him by his partner David Furnish was titled *Tantrums and Tiaras*. He once flew back from France, where one of his four properties is located, because a member of the public had the temerity to wave at him and call out a greeting while he was playing tennis. Elton John's fiftieth birthday party is best remembered for the great man making his entrance dressed like a parody of the Sun King, Louis XIV, in a silver pompadoured wig piled so high that he had to arrive in an articulated truck; no mere conventional saloon car could contain him. To put it charitably, he might have thought to parade his fame and his vast wealth with a little more sensitivity; but self-absorption of this degree is almost impossible to penetrate.

And even a modicum of knowledge about one's own self-absorption cannot quite protect famous people from falling into its trap. My conversations with actor Hugh Grant, an intelligent, eloquent man who often conceals his private feelings behind a mask of droll insouciance, reveal an ambivalent attitude towards his own celebrity.

Within months of becoming an international star in the 1994 film *Four Weddings and a Funeral*, he felt he had adjusted to fame: 'On balance, I'm loving it really. After years and years of obscurity, it would be nonsense to pretend a little bit of glamour and attention wasn't quite nice.'

Five years later, on the set of *Notting Hill*, a film that specifically deals with how fame affects private lives, his attitude was somewhat different: 'My experience has been that in England 60 per cent or 70 per cent of people are genuinely as cool about fame as the people in this film. Although they're excited to meet a star, they're not up your arse, it doesn't mean that much. It's fun for five minutes. But there's another 30 per cent who are very excited by it. It rattles and over-excites them, and they have to tell all their friends.'

And did that in turn rattle him? 'It's slightly less attractive. I don't like people shrugging it off because my ego quite likes a little bit of attention. But some get over-excited, yes, especially those friends and relations you were never particularly close to, who want to invite you to every tea party and christening. That can be galling.'

Between those two conversations, Grant had had cause to regret the fact he was internationally famous. In 1995, in Los Angeles, he was arrested with a prostitute named Divine Brown in his car on Sunset Boulevard late one night. Both pleaded no contest to charges of lewd conduct. It was a routine misdemeanour, and something very similar happens every night of the week on that particular stretch of Sunset. But because of Grant's fame, someone in the Los Angeles Police Department had the opportunistic presence of mind to leak the story to the media, along with mug shots of Grant in custody.

It was a huge entertainment industry story: Hugh Grant, the charming, diffident, exquisitely courteous romantic hero from *Four Weddings and a Funeral*, consorting with a hooker. And it had consequences. A minor one was that Divine Brown received her fifteen minutes of fame, acquiring a manager who vainly tried to hustle film deals for her on the strength of the incident. As for Grant, his public humiliation was complete, and compounded by the fact he was in the middle of publicizing a forthcoming film, the innocuous comedy *Nine Months*. He was persuaded to apologize swiftly, unreservedly and publicly for his lapse, and did so on American TV's *The Tonight Show*; acknowledging the hurt feelings of his long-time girlfriend Elizabeth Hurley, Grant admitted his behaviour had been 'swinish', in response to the memorable question the show's host Jay Leno posed to him: 'What were you thinking?'

Almost certainly, of course, Grant wasn't thinking at all. If he had been, he would surely have foreseen the strong possibility of subsequent events actually happening. Fame is a peculiar condition. It can sometimes make celebrities believe consequences that apply to other people do not apply to them at all. Such a form of narcissism often turns out to be justified; fame can be a protective shield that masks or excuses aberrant or anti-social behaviour. But in this case, the truth was the exact reverse; Grant's fame was the sole factor for the unhappy events that unravelled.

Psychologists Andrew Evans and Glenn D. Wilson have noted that such self-absorption is common among performers and actors: 'Performing breeds self-consciousness in that a requirement of the art is to see oneself as others see one. This is tantamount to holding an imaginary mirror in front of oneself. The self-consciousness that is elevated by these experiences may not be identical to narcissism, but can certainly contribute to it.'

If only self-absorption were the worst by-product of fame. Unattractive it may be, but suicide is in a different league. As detailed with lip-smacking relish by Kenneth Anger in his lurid but compelling *Hollywood Babylon* volumes, the 'magic of self-murder' by movie stars has been a subject of fascination for fans since the medium was invented. 'They had money and fame, everything we wanted,' Anger writes. 'And it still wasn't enough. They must have been sick.' He goes on to list those suicides who could not face losing their health, their youth or their beauty, quoting actress Pier Angeli who took an overdose of barbiturates at the age of thirty-nine because 'being forty would be the end of everything'. Anger has done his homework diligently, listing the truly famous (George Sanders, Marilyn Monroe, Jean Seberg, the original Superman George Reeves, Gig Young, Charles Boyer, Dorothy Dandridge, Alan Ladd and Margaret Sullavan) along with long-forgotten names.

Two things strike you about Anger's litany. One is the disproportionately high number of actors and actresses in Hollywood who have taken their lives. The other is that even a minor degree of fame strips them of posthumous dignity. Would anyone remember the name of Mexican actress Lupe Velez, if not for the circumstances of her death in 1944? Deep in debt and pregnant by a lover, she created a shrine to herself in her bedroom, with a huge mass of flowers and several dozen candles. She donned a silver lamé gown, swallowed seventy-five Seconal tablets, and lay down to die. Instead she threw up, rushed to the bathroom, slipped on the tiles and plunged head first into the toilet, where her maid found her the next morning. Most people only know Velez's name because of this story, and cannot name a single film in which she appeared.

Of course, some of these star suicides might have exhibited tendencies to unstable behaviour even if they had worked as accountants or nurses. And one can argue that the high risks and massive rewards built into a star system might attract personality types who are driven to an extraordinary extent or less grounded than their peers. It is also the case that thousands of people have had a taste of fame, and have watched it recede from their lives without entertaining suicidal thoughts.

Still, it can be a profoundly unsettling experience – an emotional equivalent of being led up to the top of a mountain, shown the view down below, then forcibly guided away from the summit. A friend of Margaux Hemingway, the actress and granddaughter of author Ernest Hemingway, who committed suicide at forty-one, having suffered problems with drugs, alcohol, eating disorders and a string of abusive relationships, said: 'She was just a gentle soul who got lost in fame and fortune.' Such is the promise that fame holds in our culture that its disappearance can be shattering. People will often do whatever they can to hold on to any vestige of it.

In the 1980s, a ventriloquist named Keith Harris was a nationally known name in Britain. He had his own TV show, largely aimed at children, on which he co-starred with his two 'talking' soft toy creations, Orville and Cuddles. Eventually, his career began to wane, and he fell back on live appearances – sometimes doing a 'blue' version of his original act. But nothing could bring him back to his former glories, and even more desperate remedies were required. Harris finally joined a touring bill of lookalikes – averagely talented people bearing some resemblance to famous performers, who could do passable impersonations of them singing or telling jokes. The twist was that Harris went out on stage as a look-alike of himself. One can only imagine what it must do to one's sense of identity, feeling obliged to appear in public pretending to be a simulacrum of oneself. But what does it say about our culture and our curious attitude to celebrity that people are prepared to pay good money to see a lookalike, but not the original? Irony has much to answer for when customers take pleasure in watching a performer they would not dream of paying to see in his own right pretending to impersonate himself.

If Harris was always a minor figure, the tragic career arc of Orson Welles is one of the saddest, longest and most monumental. Since his stunning emergence as a Hollywood wunderkind in 1941 with *Citizen Kane*, still regarded in most critics' polls as the greatest film ever made, his reputation suffered an agonizingly long, slow decline. When he died in 1985 obituarists portrayed him as a has-been.

Two years before his death, I used to encounter Welles regularly. I was living in Los Angeles, and had taken a job as Hollywood bureau chief for a newly-launched entertainment magazine with multi-million dollar backing. Part of my brief was to wine and dine film studio bosses and TV network chiefs, enthuse about the magazine, and pick up the bill.

That summer, the place they all wanted to go was Ma Maison, an expensive French eaterie on Melrose Avenue run by Patrick Terrail, a publicity-hungry chef. It was then a favoured hangout for Hollywood glitterati: Nicholson, Eastwood, Streisand and Lemmon were regulars. But the constant presence – Banquo's ghost at the feast – was Welles. He ate lunch alone at a side table, staring balefully out into the power crowd, daring any of them to meet his gaze. None did. Transfixed by this spectre, I would nudge my companions and point him out. Invariably they looked away and rapidly changed the subject. Nearing seventy by then and grossly overweight, Welles was perceived as washed up, so uncommercial and temperamental that no studio executive would even deign to take a meeting with him. Independent financiers sometimes hatched wild schemes for new films, but they always seemed to fall at the final hurdle: no one would take the risk of allowing Welles ever to direct again. Shamefully, this prodigiously talented figure had become a pariah, a figure of fun best known as the fat man who hawked California wine on TV commercials in hammy, sonorous tones; he used to make them, according to his biographer Barbara Leaming, to pay for groceries.

Over about six months of that year, Welles and I saw enough of each other at Ma Maison to be on nodding terms. He knew I was clearly no Hollywood executive, and when he spied me he would tilt his giant head, rolling his eyes conspiratorially in mocking disdain at all the wheeler-dealers in the restaurant. Ironically, his career enjoyed a posthumous vogue some fifteen years later; a whole new generation of Hollywood executives and film-makers who knew nothing of his long decline simply responded to his best work: *Citizen Kane*, *The Magnificent Ambersons* – and *Touch of Evil*, heavily cut by Universal Pictures on its release in 1958 but lovingly restored to its original form in 1999. Some of these young bloods fancied themselves as rebellious young prodigies, and saw in Welles the same attitude and qualities. For him, of course, this resurgence came way too late.

Yet the transient nature of fame is only one of its potential downsides. Enough of these have been recorded to become routine. Marilyn Monroe (who, remember, committed suicide) once observed that fame 'is not what fulfils you. When you're famous, every weakness is exaggerated.' Katharine Hepburn once remarked: 'Fame gave me everything – except what I wanted.' The 1980s rock star Pat Benatar once told an interviewer she was desperate at age twenty-two to become famous, indifferent at twenty-six, and by the age of twenty-eight had come to detest fame. The British character actor Michael Maloney has noted: 'Anyone who craves fame is not aware of the consequences.'

The price that fame exerts has even been enshrined in a line of Shakespeare's: 'King Henry the Fifth, too famous to live long!' But the notion easily predates Shakespeare: Homer's *Iliad* contains a passage in which Achilles is told the price of his glory is a short life, a fact that embitters him; and in the *Odyssey*, Achilles is to be found in the underworld, the fame he attained on earth totally irrelevant.

Given these pitfalls and warnings, why do so many people strive to achieve fame? Possibly because all its alluring aspects are visible and obvious – the tip of the iceberg above the water line – and all its drawbacks are hidden. It is evident that wealth may well accompany fame (if not necessarily). Equally it is clear that fame carries with it a certain sexual magnetism, endowing its bearers with a charisma they might not otherwise be seen to possess. One sees that the applause and adulation of an audience might induce feelings of triumph and a sense of power beyond their imaginings.

And that is part of the trouble, of course. Fame truly is beyond the imaginings of people who have yet to experience it. It also changes their attitudes, their priorities and their value systems in an unforeseeable manner; effectively, this produces a shift in identity that can be hugely disorienting.

No figure in contemporary pop culture exemplifies this better than Michael Jackson. It's sad now to watch old TV clips of him as a child star performing with his brothers; singing 'I Want You Back' or 'ABC', he looked a bubbly, joyous little Afro-American boy with talent to burn.

THE PITFALLS OF FAME

In 1983, I was in the audience for the televised *Motown 25* concert, celebrating his record label's longevity. It was an arduous night stretching over five hours, with interminable breaks between various Motown acts as sets were wheeled on and off stage for the TV cameras. But Jackson's performance was absolutely electrifying; this was the night he seized the imagination of the pop world with his astonishing moonwalk dance. He was in his mid-twenties then, at the peak of his powers, dynamic, sublimely gifted and still recognizably black. Within a year his album *Thriller*, and a series of jolting videos from it, confirmed him as (the title he and his advisers preferred) the King of Pop.

From that point onwards, everything seemed to go wrong. Jackson's career has been marked not only by his music but by his descent into what looks like melancholy neurosis. The pigmentation of his skin changed gradually until he came to resemble a white man. Plastic surgery transformed his face, obliterating any suggestion of Afro-American features. He had two short-lived marriages; the first, to Elvis Presley's daughter Lisa Marie, rated as one of the most surely doomed unions in show business annals. Jackson was the subject of allegations of child molesting, which were finally settled out of court. He declared a fascination – a morbid one, it could be agreed – with neurological operations. He often appears in public with his pet chimpanzee Bubbles. Just as often he has been seen wearing a mask over his mouth, or carrying his own oxygen tank. He is intrigued by the story of Peter Pan – unsurprising for one inhabiting his own personal Neverland.

In short, Jackson parades his own psychological problems for all to see. Reportedly his father Joe had a stormy relationship with Michael, beating him and insisting that he rehearse and perform, sometimes against his will, before he was five years old. In 2001 Jackson, before his infamous address to the Oxford Union, said of his father: 'He never told me he loved me.' But in the same address he described Joe as 'a managerial genius' – an intriguing comment from a man who has subsequently changed managers frequently.

Everything one needs to know about Michael Jackson's celebrity status is contained in the invitation for him to speak at the Oxford Union. Jackson took as his text the need to protect the children of the world, and at one point seemed so overcome that he was close to tears. Few thought to point out the grisly conjunction of this address and the child-abuse allegations against him eight years previously; and if there were any in the student body opposed to the invitation, their feelings were not vented publicly. Even the Oxford Union, it seemed, could be so dazzled by fame that it could take a morally neutral view of celebrities.

In fact Jackson's behaviour, when removed from the curious environment of fame where different standards apply, looks simply bizarre. Any unnamed obscure person exhibiting these external traits would surely be urged to seek psychiatric help. But here is where fame becomes a trap. Jackson's career might have lost some of its lustre, but he remains a considerable economic powerhouse: and who in his entourage will tell him that his behaviour is alarming, that he needs help? He needs a jester in his court, a dissenter in his retinue.

In this sense Jackson resembles his predecessor as the King of Pop, Elvis Presley, who also had no idea what to do with his global fame. He would spend long evenings at Graceland bored senseless, surrounded by the Memphis Mafia, his unlovely collection of hangers-on; their role was to laugh uproariously at the King's feeble jokes, pour him drinks, watch TV with him and observe him becoming bloated on pills and junk food. Not one of them warned Presley he was on the skids, and maybe endangering his life. Why would they? Why risk incurring his disaffection and being cast out of the mansion? It wasn't as if any of them had a range of alternative career options.

Still, it is pointless to be judgemental about the styles of life celebrities choose for themselves. Fame is an uncharted terrain for any individual, and there are no useful precedents or rulebooks that suggest how it might best be negotiated, especially when the degree of fame experienced is as intense as Presley's and Jackson's. And when an uncertainty about how to behave is accompanied by a lack of pressure to conform to the same standards as ordinary people, it is hard to maintain a sense of identity and equilibrium.

This may be why famous people appear to make a habit of congregating together; fame sets them apart from others and at least in celebrity company there may be common ground. In this context, obscure people can almost seem threatening. Clive James recalls walking into a Hollywood party where every face was famous except his own: 'That hadn't happened for years. Someone they didn't know hadn't got that close. Paul Newman practically reached for his gun. It was a very small world they all inhabited, and necessarily so.' But London-based psychotherapist Nan Beecher-Moore insists that for people uneasy with their fame, cultivating the company of other celebrities is a false refuge: 'They're not true peers. When you're with other famous people, they're just as phoney as you feel you are.'

Fame, in fact, appears to have a knack of exacerbating the problems of those who were troubled already. When Paula Yates, the British TV presenter, ex-wife of Bob Geldof and lover of rock singer Michael Hutchence, died in 2000 from a drug overdose, obituarists were quick to point to her troubled past. They noted her loveless childhood, the fact that the man she grew up considering her father turned out not to be, and Hutchence's own bizarre death three years previously. In the latter years of her life she had suffered a nervous breakdown and spent time in a drug rehabilitation programme. Yates, one writer affirmed, was murdered by 'a lethal substance called celebrity'. And the journalist Yvonne Roberts wrote: 'For our entertainment we watch as a mentally ill individual "blessed" by fame disintegrates before us.' It almost goes without saying that in her earlier, obscure days, Yates seemed to those who met her to be avidly interested in the pursuit of her own celebrity.

The consequences of fame are not always as tragic; but it frequently exerts lesser costs. There are whole ranks of performers who decide at some stage of their careers to re-invent themselves, to present a whole new face to the public, and effectively obliterate their previous identities. This does not really apply to performers like David Bowie or Madonna, who have in the past used a process of constant re-invention for quasi-artistic purposes. But among less talented performers, there exists a more desperate form of re-invention, born out of a slowing of career momentum. It often happens in the world of pop music, where performers jettison singing styles, modify their on-stage attitudes and even change their appearance, all in pursuit of an often imaginary new audience.

The subtext to all this can be summarized thus: 'You no longer like me that way, will you like me this way?' In career terms, it may just be a last despairing, if commercially justifiable, roll of the dice; but in terms of an individual identity, what does it say? It says such performers care more about clinging on to fame at any cost, rather than sticking with the more 'authentic' persona or the natural gifts that helped them become famous in the first place.

A good example of this tendency is ex-Spice Girl Geri Halliwell. Anyone who met the group in their heyday came away convinced of two things: that she was the natural leader, and of all five members probably the least concerned about her image. She was breezy, spirited, saucy and good fun. The Spice Girls were clearly ambitious, but she seemed refreshingly free of neuroses, and did not appear to take herself terribly seriously. She was the one who would pinch the bottoms of male backstage visitors, a privilege which was even extended to Prince Charles. Her trademark outfit was an unsubtle mini-dress with a Union Jack pattern.

But when Halliwell left the group after a bout of internal squabbles, she took it upon herself to transform every detail of her image. She embarked on a solo career and suddenly became deadly serious. She lost weight dramatically, using a course of vitamin injections to resculpt her body; newly svelte, she bid farewell to her former bouncy brashness. Her formerly reddish hair now became discreetly blonde; she assumed a new public service role, working with the United Nations to promote 'issues of reproductive health'. In this capacity, she took to wearing sober outfits in grey, navy and black; the overall effect was not exactly convincing. She talked blithely of moving into films, but nothing came of it. In short, she had dumped the old Geri and with the help of public relations advisers morphed herself into a totally different creature. Her solo records initially sold well, but if future sales falter, what then? In terms of her own identity, she seemed to be painting herself into a corner. And it is noticeable that the new super-slim Halliwell looks far more ill-at-ease than the original model.

One can make a case that she and other obsessive re-inventors like her are victims of fame and its addictive qualities. But the damage it causes can be collateral as well as direct; as any child of a famous parent will attest, the constant unfavourable comparisons can be demoralizing. One of the great examples here is Frank Sinatra Jr., who was kidnapped at the age of nineteen in 1976, and only released for a ransom of $240,000 – simply because of who his father was. He has since spent his adult life in that long shadow as a singer, composer and musical arranger; but has anyone ever sat through a Frank Sinatra Jr. show without mentally comparing father and son?

Despite the promise it holds out for happiness, or what Professor Csikszentmihalyi would call an optimal experience, fame is a distinctly thorny business. Since embarking on this book, friends and acquaintances have asked whether I would enjoy being famous – or as they usually phrase it, 'rich and famous'. I have started to tell them that I would have no objection to being rich, as long as my wealth could remain reasonably secret. But fame, no: it simply doesn't seem worth the burden. Even such a skilled manipulator of private and public personae as David Bowie knows its downside, as he told artist Tracey Emin in a published conversation: 'I certainly fancied my spoonful of it when I was young. I was more than downcast to find that fame brought nothing more than good seats in a restaurant. There is nothing there to covet ... so I won't be recommending it to my offspring.' Bowie neglected to add that no matter how shrewdly one negotiates the terms and conditions of one's fame, once attained, it is a commodity with which one is never alone.

11
Privacy

RULE ELEVEN:
You cannot court celebrity purely on your own terms

One of the most enduring sequences of television footage of Diana, Princess of Wales shows her trying to walk down a London street with paparazzi dogging her every step. She is visibly distressed; her large solemn eyes are brimming with tears. Oblivious to her discomfort, or more likely galvanized by it, the photographers keep snapping away at her. At one point, Diana lifts an arm to shield the side of her face. It is as if she is cowering under a hail of physical blows. The imagery evoked in this sequence is deeply unsettling; she looks like an abused child.

The actress Nicole Kidman told me that dealing with paparazzi is the single hardest aspect of her fame: 'They can become unbearable. You don't want to be photographed every time you walk your kids in the park, or buy a newspaper. I don't have any desire to be on TV every moment of my life. But whether you want it or not, they're there and they don't stop.' Kidman conveyed the sensation of feeling under siege by imitating the noise of flashbulbs popping: 'Pow! Pow! Pow!'

This experience can leave celebrities feeling battered. Even Madonna, who has in the past actively participated in blurring divisions between her public and personal life, now feels worn down by the constant attentions of the paparazzi, and has expressed a desire for privacy.

Unauthorized pictures taken by paparazzi have severe limitations: they are literally snapshots in time, but the media can employ them to underscore any number of spurious theses about celebrities. Actress Calista Flockhart, whose weight and diet have been obsessively recorded in the press, neatly summarizes this tendency: 'Not having anonymity makes you feel so scrutinized. Back home, I can go to a grocery store and squeeze a grapefruit, and suddenly there are reports that I have an obsession with grapefruit.'

When another actress, Kate Winslet, separated from her husband Jim Threapleton, a photograph of her returning home with her baby daughter ran in the *Daily Telegraph*. An accompanying caption, written by a journalist at his desk, claimed that the photograph showed clear signs of the strain and pressure she was suffering. Did it? Or did the camera merely catch her that way? Could another photograph from the same sheet, maybe with Winslet flashing a grin, have been used to make precisely the opposite claim? We shall never know; but certainly making such sweeping public assumptions about individuals on the basis of a snatched photograph is a secondary invasion of their privacy.

It is easy to make paparazzi the scapegoats in the uneasy conflict between famous people who wish to retain some degree of privacy and a public, represented by the media, who seek more gossip, more private detail, more scurrilous facts and sensational pictures. We have all seen enough of their methods to feel some distaste towards them: they can by pushy, rude and intrusive. The finger of guilt in the immediate wake of Diana's death was initially pointed at those paparazzi who chased her car down that tunnel in Paris, their own vehicles speeding crazily like some vengeful posse determined to hunt her down.

Yet the paparazzi are merely the shock troops in this war, the element that reinforces to celebrities the unpleasantness of encroachments on their privacy. To use a more specific metaphor, they are front line mercenaries, doing what they do only to earn a living. And they earn a living – in some cases, a lucrative one – only because newspaper and magazine editors will buy their photographs of celebrities caught in private, distressed or compromised circumstances, often turning a blind eye to the means that achieved this end.

Let us blame the media, then. But of course the media are merely surrogates to the public will: photographs, gossip and revelations that the famous would prefer to keep private have become a means of selling certain types of newspapers and magazines. Indeed, their thwarted preference for privacy becomes a selling tool; their unwillingness to play ball with this part of the publicity process, and their palpable distress at the intrusion, adds a frisson to perusing such accounts in the press. They take on a forbidden quality. That frequently used phrase, 'the pictures X and Y didn't want you to see', becomes its own justification. No consideration is given to why any reader, merely for his or her own minor titillation, would want to collude in such infractions of an individual's privacy.

Recently, celebrities have started hitting back, seeking redress through the courts against those who would infringe their privacy. Several famous people have successfully taken action against stalkers and those who persistently harass them, often obtaining injunctions or restraining orders that prevent such people from approaching them.

The more intriguing area in terms of privacy, though, is the relationship between famous people and the media, especially as it relates to unauthorized photographs. Historically, the media have taken the view that the famous are fair game if they are on public property: just as it is not unlawful for private individuals to point cameras wherever they wish while on public property, so the media can photograph celebrities, no matter what activity they are engaged in.

However, some celebrities have sought to challenge this sense of automatic right. The 'supermodel' Naomi Campbell was so incensed that the *Mirror* published a story and pictures of her attending a south London meeting of the therapy group Narcotics Anonymous that she sued the newspaper and in 2002 won the modest damages of £3,500 in the High Court. Yet Mr Justice Morland upheld the *Mirror*'s right to publish the story and pictures because of her earlier denials of her drug problems; the damages were for publishing additional details, 'sensitive personal data' as he put it, that she would have wished to remain secret. The Campbell case was significant, because judges were at least prepared to place a limit on the extent of media intrusion into celebrities' lives. Actors Michael Douglas and Catherine Zeta-Jones took similar action against the glossy magazine *Hello!* after 'unauthorized' pictures of their wedding in New York found their way into its pages. BBC radio disc jockey Sara Cox sued for invasion of privacy after covertly taken pictures of her on honeymoon, naked beside the swimming pool of a secluded villa in the Seychelles, appeared in the *Sunday People*.

Before 2000, these people might not have felt emboldened to pursue their grievances in the courts. But in that year the European Human

Rights Act, which enshrines an individual's right to privacy, came into force in Britain, a country where it has the potential to make a huge difference. This is not true everywhere. In France, for instance, where rigorous privacy laws have long existed, it is illegal to publish photographs of people without permission.

Built-in contradictions exist within the Act, which suggests the battle between media seeking full disclosure and celebrities guarding their privacy will be protracted. One Article declares an individual has 'the right to respect for his private and family life, his home and correspondence', while the next but one asserts 'the right to freedom of expression, freedom to hold opinions and to receive and impart information and ideas without interference by public authority'. There is comfort in those clauses for the famous and the media respectively, but it seems likely in future that celebrities will use the Act as a means of preventing material about them that they regard as unfavourable or unflattering from being published.

Yet is it equally likely that the media will fight their corner, citing the importance of a public-interest defence in being free to publish. In some cases, it is hard to deny that they have a point. Douglas and Zeta-Jones, for instance, could hardly claim their wedding-day privacy was sacrosanct; they had already auctioned it off in an exclusive £1 million deal to *OK!*, a rival magazine to *Hello!*. But what made the photographs in *Hello!* doubly galling to the couple and to *OK!* was that they appeared a full three days before *OK!* appeared on the newsstands. Douglas and Zeta-Jones might well argue that little public interest is served in *Hello!* publishing their photographs; yet celebrities like them actively pursue publicity for which there is equally scant public interest when they have something they wish to promote.

Clearly the French privacy laws are too all-encompassing to be satisfactory, and sometimes hamper the dissemination of important information. The case routinely cited is President Mitterrand, who was suffering from cancer through almost the entire term of his presidency. This was a fact with political and constitutional implications; had it been widely known, it would have cast new light on his ability to perform his duties.

Yet contrast the fortunes of two American presidents, Kennedy and Clinton, both of whom involved themselves with women other than their wives. Kennedy acceded to the White House in a pre-Watergate era when the media still kept inside knowledge of a president's personal foibles to themselves. They knew of his many dalliances, winked confidentially and published nothing: it remained a secret within the Beltway. Clinton's presidency coincided with a high-watermark of desire for full disclosure on the part of the media, even when such disclosure hinged on speculation and gossip. This created an atmosphere in which he could be brought to the verge of impeachment, and the Starr Report could record with a voyeur's relish every last detail of his Oval Office trysts with the intern Monica Lewinsky.

But in retrospect, on which occasion was the American public interest better served? The knowledge of Kennedy's obsessive womanizing would certainly have tarnished his gilded reputation. In the short term, it may also have led him to be appraised differently as a president. In the late 1960s, it was often conveniently overlooked that the charismatic Kennedy, rather than his far less attractive successor Lyndon Johnson, first engaged American troops in Vietnam; and that Johnson's, not Kennedy's, administration did most of the spadework involved in civil rights legislation. Kennedy's voting record as a senator before he became President actually shows him less liberal than is fondly imagined in hazy recollection.

As for Clinton, a lack of public knowledge about his affairs would merely have removed a stick with which his political enemies might beat him. Did both men behave badly while in office? Without question. Clinton's weaselly description of his dalliance with Lewinsky as 'inappropriate' fails to do justice to its gravity. Yet no one has seriously claimed that either man's extramarital pursuits ever affected their work as President of the United States, nor swayed any decisions they made. The worst one can say is that too much of Clinton's time was diverted from pressing world matters and spent managing the fallout from his sexual liaisons, which included Gennifer Flowers, Paula Jones and certainly others before Lewinsky. In the end, it seemed Kennedy got away with it during his lifetime, while Clinton was revealed as he was, a man with a specific weakness.

But let us remember that during World War II the future President Eisenhower, in public a model of old-fashioned, even dull, rectitude, had a mistress of long standing, who did double duty as his army driver. Insiders in the press corps knew it, but reported not a word. Media coyness was not limited to sexual matters. Franklin D. Roosevelt was stricken by polio, which left him unable to stand without leg braces and largely confined him to a wheelchair for years; but during his presidency most Americans remained ignorant of the fact.

Looking back half a century or more at Eisenhower and Roosevelt, we may find those matters intriguing; but it is hard to claim that they affected anything of political or military importance. In retrospect, do we feel duped by them? Most of us do not. The errant behaviour of Kennedy and Clinton is more jarring mainly because they are more recent historical figures. But it does not quite make them charlatans; one would have to study their public pronouncements long and hard for evidence of hypocrisy or deception.

Of all famous people, it is elected politicians who must adhere most closely to a set of standards, which in fairness they understand before embarking on their journey to fame. (No one can be naïve enough to run for President or Prime Minister without realizing they are also seeking fame.) Being elected implies accepting a contract with the electorate that must not be breached. Thus politicians should clearly not preach against or advocate legislation against behaviour that they practise in private; nor should they seek personal gain through the tenure of public office.

But do today's standards leave them room for any privacy? One might ideally wish politicians to be models of probity, restraint and fidelity, but it is setting the bar too high to insist their past lives must always have been so spotless. Few people who live gregarious lives reach the sort of age when they might be considered for high political office without having something to hide – or, to be precisely accurate, something they would prefer not to be publicly known. It is virtually a definition of what privacy entails. It would be a dull, unimaginative life that did not include some youthful indiscretion, a lapse of judgement or less than praiseworthy behaviour.

Yet politicians' early lives are routinely dredged for evidence of bad faith, malfeasance and even hot-headedness; the process places them in a bind that does nothing to help a democratic process. This tendency reached a nadir when Clinton was asked about his use of marijuana during his student days. Forced to say he had smoked it (otherwise some witness might have been found to nail his lie) he added in mitigation that he did not inhale, a statement that was irrefutable. Irrefutable, but completely preposterous.

Given the scope of these enquiries, one might venture that no modern politician could withstand such scrutiny. Increasingly, able people have ruled out a political career for themselves because the jeopardy of exposure is not worth the trouble. And that suggests that the informal standards used to determine suitability for public office, with the media drawing ever-shifting lines in the sand, are misjudged.

The media, of course, have much to gain from aiming for an excess of disclosure, even when it means trampling on an individual's privacy; a series of lurid revelations sells newspapers and keeps viewers glued to TV news broadcasts. With politicians especially, the media can plead full disclosure is 'in the public interest', a phrase that more and more comes to mean 'something the public is interested in'. That is not the same thing at all.

In the early 1990s, the British Conservative Cabinet minister David Mellor was found to have had an affair with Antonia de Sancha, an unemployed actress. She found a publicist, who sold her story to the tabloid press; it included the revelation that Mellor liked to have sex while wearing a football shirt in the colours of Chelsea, the team he famously supported. The British press fell upon this item with glee, and it was widely repeated, though few within the media seriously believed it; clearly it is a tongue-in-cheek parody of a wish-list tabloid headline, incorporating readers' favourite interests: sex, football and a politician caught behaving badly. The headline had another virtue in the eyes of the tabloids: it was so scurrilous and absurd that a senior politician like Mellor could not dignify it with any response (even a denial) without making himself look even more of a laughing stock.

In the end, no public interest was served – it was just a joke at which the British could snigger. No thought was given to how it might wound those close to him. In fairness Mellor did not help his case, swiftly arranging a photo call of himself posing with his wife and children, all looking distinctly strained. It was a cynical exercise aimed at portraying him as a steadfast husband and family man, and it backfired. He was widely attacked for hypocrisy. Later he divorced, re-married and resigned from the Cabinet; the Chelsea shirt incident was held to have contributed to his downfall. Mellor is a hard man to sympathize with, especially as he was part of a Tory Government then advocating 'family values'. But did he deserve to have intimate details (or, more likely, inventions) about his private life dragged into the open and held up for public mockery?

The same applies to President Clinton and his liaisons; there was a furtive, repetitive pattern to them, and it was bad behaviour for a man who was also leader of the free world. Yet the worst one can say about him is that he misused his powerful position, first as Governor of Arkansas and then as US President, to press his attentions on these women. He broke no laws. And while it might be useful for the American electorate to know that Clinton was a philanderer, there were surely limits to that useful knowledge. What purpose, for instance, was served by the revelations about the presidential semen on Monica Lewinsky's dress? True, it gave Clinton's political opponents lip-smacking delight; it helped sell acres of newsprint with sensational headlines, thrilled executives of TV networks with news broadcasts, and gave much of the free world plenty to gossip about. But it was a sleazy, unnecessary exercise that demeaned everyone involved: independent counsel Kenneth Starr's team of investigators, Lewinsky, Clinton and the office of the presidency – even more than Clinton himself had demeaned it by his behaviour in the Oval Office. Above all, the incident signalled that civilized standards of privacy no longer applied. As an interesting footnote, Clinton's popularity ratings did not slump as a result of these disclosures but were slightly enhanced, possibly because of a public backlash against his enemies who brought them into the open.

Since the scandal in the White House, Lewinsky has been outspoken and vocal about the invasion of her privacy. In her liaison with Clinton, she sought no fame and committed no crime; her name would be obscure to this day had not Paula Jones accused Clinton of unwanted advances and filed a sexual harassment suit against him. Jeffrey Rosen, author of *The Unwanted Gaze*, which deals with the rapid diminishing of privacy in America, has noted: 'Merely by accusing Clinton of an unwanted advance, Jones was able to violate not only his privacy but also that of Monica Lewinsky, who was forced to describe her own consensual sexual activities under oath.'

In fact her entire private life was held up to scrutiny by Starr and his team. He decided to subpoena a Washington bookstore for receipts of all her purchases in the previous two years. Prosecutors were allowed to search her house and retrieve from her personal computer love letters to Clinton she had composed but never sent. As Rosen observes: 'In the late eighteenth century, the spectacle of state agents breaking into a suspect's home and rummaging through his or her private diaries was considered the paradigm case of the unreasonable searches and seizures that the framers of the Bill of Rights intended to forbid.'

According to Lewinsky's biographer Andrew Morton, when she protested to one of Starr's deputies about the seizure of the unsent letters, she was told they would be placed under lock and key, and might not even appear in Starr's report to Congress. Of course, Starr did include them in his report, which Congress duly made available on the Internet for all to read.

Lewinsky's problems did not stop with Paula Jones's lawyers or Kenneth Starr and his team. The American media declared open season on her personal life, hunting down every morsel of information it could find from her twenty-two-year life, and tracking down even remote acquaintances of hers from school for any recollections. They were helped in their task by the fact that Lewinsky was effectively gagged: in return for an immunity deal with Starr's office, she was legally forbidden to discuss most aspects of the case. Effectively she could not put her side of the story to the press, even while aides for Clinton and Starr were busy leaking and spinning, suggesting avenues of inquiry that would place their bosses in a favourable light. As a result, according to Frank Rich of the *New York Times*, 'she had no choice but to remain silent even as her image and her story morphed into profit centres for the entertainment industry.'

In other words, the media invented the characteristics for Lewinsky that were most convenient, most saleable. 'Once the name and the picture were out there,' she told Rich, 'then it was "let's start giving her attributes and start forming her as a person". Everything was scrutinized and analysed by the TV psychologists, and the persona was created.' Unsurprisingly, this persona was not a complex one; Lewinsky was portrayed as a stereotypically dumb bimbo, the kind rich, powerful politicians inevitably seem to fall for. Understandably, she found the characterization offensive, but once set in stone it was impossible to modify; the media wanted to hear nothing about her that would complicate or ruin the overall 'story' they had constructed. And predictably those sections of the press for which cheque-book journalism is a routine way of doing business paid higher fees to informants who had cruel, negative or sensational items of gossip about Lewinsky's past to sell.

It is particularly helpful if the famous person under scrutiny is in no position to respond to criticism. Lewinsky, legally gagged, was a helpless victim. But the British Royal Family are even more obvious sitting targets; protocol and tradition forbids them to respond directly to criticisms or scurrilous stories about them. During the 1960s and 1970s, the British press had treated the Royals with a degree of deference that masked an underlying lack of interest; but then Prince Charles found himself a bride in the shape of shy, lovely young Diana Spencer, and all hell was let loose. From the announcement of her engagement to Charles until well after her death, Diana could shift papers and magazines off newsstands and attract mass TV audiences like no other human being on earth. She was a gift to the media, which accrued untold fortunes based on the display of her image.

With stakes this high, it was clear that any proprieties about privacy would soon evaporate. And so it happened. Diana quickly cottoned on to the fact that she was now a public figure, and part of her did not altogether like the role. (The other part of her liked it only too well.) The couple set about producing two sons, by which time their paths had diverged; succession to the throne secured, they seemed to have little left to say to each other. And their life together was made hugely more unpleasant by an unparalleled degree of intrusiveness by both the media and the public. Being globally famous, Charles and Diana might just about have imagined that someone would try to intercept and monitor their private phone conversations with others; but because there was no precedent for this degree of intrusion, they might not have imagined that transcripts of those conversations would end up on the front pages of British newspapers. Diana might have conceded the possibility that even in her gym she was not safe from a snooper with a camera; she would not have predicted that he would turn out to be the gym manager, nor that a national paper would be found to splash his ill-gotten photos of her working out in a leotard.

The Royal Family has traditionally stood on its dignity in the face of such unwarranted intrusions on its privacy. So an incident that occurred in 2001, when Charles and Diana's son Prince William arrived for his first year of studies at St Andrews University in Scotland, proved to be a source of huge amusement. William's arrival caused a huge buzz of media interest. But after an initial arranged photo call of the prince, the press discreetly retreated, upholding a six-year code of agreement between themselves, the Press Complaints Commission and the Windsors, drawn up to protect Princes William and Harry from long-lens intrusion.

Yet one camera crew lingered at St Andrews, continuing to film for three days after being asked to withdraw; to the utter embarrassment of the monarchy, the crew turned out to belong to Ardent, a production company run by Prince Edward, the Earl of Wessex, William's uncle. The incident almost defied belief, especially as Edward himself had previously complained about media intrusion. But there was a serious question lurking behind all the humorous comment about it: if members of the Windsors could not restrain themselves in the interests of Prince William's privacy, how could the family complain about anyone else?

Members of the Royal Family simply cannot afford to make minor mistakes like the rest of us, as seventeen-year-old Prince Harry found to his cost in 2002, when it was revealed that he had experimented with cannabis and had on more than one occasion drunk alcohol to excess. Literally millions of teenagers in Britain stumble their way through similar rites of passage, but their privacy is not infringed by seeing their misdemeanours reported on the front page of every national newspaper. (This unfortunate selectivity is not quite confined to the Royals; Tony Blair's son Euan made similar front page headlines in 2000, after being arrested for drunkenness in London's Leicester Square.)

After Charles and Diana separated, their narrative split into two, like amoebae – and both narratives were sufficiently compelling to ensure that their privacy was always likely to be under constant threat. The first held that Charles was trying to live his life quietly and with dignity, doing good works and playing a part in raising his sons, while

Diana was a loose cannon, emotionally unstable and hungry for publicity. The other narrative held that Charles, whose ardour for his old friend Camilla Parker Bowles had never quite abated, had betrayed Diana, who had been cruelly frozen out by the Queen, Prince Philip, and senior stony-faced courtiers to the House of Windsor. Among all the Royal Family, this second narrative insisted, only Diana was sufficiently in touch with her emotions to be a truly modern monarchical figure, to engage public sympathy and to raise her sons with the degree of warmth and feeling deemed appropriate by media chatterboxes.

These two parallel but conflicting versions had the potential to run almost indefinitely, and each one had several intriguing strands. Would Charles make his romance with Camilla public? Would he stand aside as heir to the throne to marry her, if necessary? Who were Diana's suitors? What would her life entail after her mauling by the Windsors? Posing any one of these questions was a good way to sell magazines, newspapers and hastily assembled TV documentaries. As a general rule, the media maintained its cavalier attitude towards royal privacy: publish first, count the profits, argue about ethics later.

This philosophy might have looked distinctly shabby but for Diana's notably ambivalent attitude towards the press. Sometimes, at times of pressure and stress, she clearly wished to be left alone. But when it suited her, she courted publicity. She identified reporters in the pack of royal correspondents who were openly sympathetic to her – Richard Kay of the *Daily Mail*, and Andrew Morton, later her biographer – and on occasions personally leaked stories to them that might place her in a favourable light. Judging herself to be in an ongoing war with the Windsors, she did not hesitate to use traditional propaganda methods; she fought her ground by allowing herself to be photographed with landmine victims and children with Aids, and letting it be known that she made 'secret' visits to the chronically sick in hospitals in the dead of night. Dazzled by this campaign, the tabloid press rewarded Diana with an approving nickname: the Queen of Hearts.

But in doing this, she failed to realize the one thing almost all famous people fail to realize: if you court celebrity, you cannot do it purely on your own terms. If you encourage the media to inspect you when you want it, they assume a right to inspect you when you do not; and your accessibility during propitious times will be used as a justification to invade your privacy at more trying times. This sombre truth finally caught up with Diana during the summer of 1997, when she was conducting a romance with Dodi Fayed, the playboy son of Mohammed al Fayed, the Egyptian multi-millionaire business tycoon and owner of Harrods. Paparazzi had taken long-lens photos of Diana in a swimsuit on board one of al Fayed's yachts with Dodi; that these photos were unwelcome to the couple did not prevent them being sold for handsome sums. So it was inevitable that paparazzi would be in evidence when the couple showed up in Paris on 31 August, and equally inevitable that they would give chase when their chauffeur made the fatal decision to try and shake them off at high speed through the city's tunnels and underpasses. Diana, who found a means to express herself in life through her own celebrity, finally died because of it, never quite appreciating that fame is not some tangible commodity that can be contained at will, but a lucrative business. For what were those paparazzi chasing? In narrow terms, of course, a picture, any picture of Diana and Dodi together. But in a broader sense, they were chasing money, vast amounts of it. When economic motives are this strong, civilized notions like individual privacy are pushed firmly into the back seat.

12

Conclusion

RULE TWELVE:
Fame is a dual-edged sword, with profound drawbacks for each of its advantages

The onward march of celebrity culture was temporarily halted in its tracks on 11 September 2001, that infamous day when planes hijacked by militant terrorists were piloted into the Pentagon and the twin towers of the World Trade Center. Thousands of people died, and so numbingly vast was the scale of the disaster that media commentators quickly ventured things would never be the same again – the human spirit, the sense of security that many of us in the West take for granted, and especially our obsession with the trivia of pop culture. A new seriousness and gravity had entered our lives, and such nonsense as the exploits of the famous-for-being-famous would no longer engage our attention: we would look for our heroes elsewhere. Graydon Carter, the editor of *Vanity Fair*, declared prematurely that he thought irony was dead, which many took to mean that in future he would think long and hard about adorning the cover of his magazine with winsome, insubstantial young actors and pop stars. (Early in 2002 Carter, taking his own cue by adopting an irony-free prose style, called the pages of *Vanity Fair* 'the High Sierra of the Public Image'.)

It didn't happen, of course. Within hours of the attacks, it was revealed that two celebrities (or near-celebrities) had perished; David Angell, the creator of the long running TV comedy series *Frasier*, and the socialite and sometime photographer Berry Berenson, the widow of *Psycho* star Anthony Perkins. No publication or TV station specifically made the case that their lives were somehow more precious than others who had died, yet they were swiftly singled out.

Still, this was inoffensive compared with what happened in the next few days. In New York, a succession of celebrities took it upon themselves to visit Ground Zero, where rescue workers were still trying to retrieve bodies from the rubble of what had once been the twin towers. Robert de Niro was among them, as was Susan Sarandon and the comic Chris Rock. In the end, Rudy Giuliani, the city's exasperated mayor, had to issue an order that celebrities must stay away; their presence was merely hampering important work.

Let us assume that the motives of these celebrities for visiting Ground Zero were blameless, and had nothing to do with favourable publicity or self-aggrandisement. It remains a terrible condemnation of modern society's distorted values that people surveying the horror of the ruins – or more importantly, working to search for trapped victims – could be stopped in their tracks, their attention diverted by the mere presence of movie actors.

The notion of profound change, the idea that nothing would ever be the same again, lasted only as long as it took for those media people with the shortest attention spans to become bored by the aftermath of 11 September. Three weeks later, the *New York Times* carried a story with the absurdly ponderous headline: 'In little time, pop culture is almost back to normal.' Yet Richard Johnson, editor of the *New York Post*'s Page Six gossip and nightlife column, had beaten the *Times* to the punch. Johnson had already greeted the post-11 September appearance in public (in a diaphanous dress) of the teenage heiress and socialite Paris Hilton as 'the first robin of spring'. His tongue was doubtless firmly in his cheek, but the comment signified how hasty and determined the world was to return to its trivial preoccupations. Carter's *Vanity Fair* rushed out a special edition to accompany its November issue with pictures of New York firefighters, nurses, trauma teams and rescue volunteers. But all were photographed with the same glamorous, stylized sheen as the magazine's traditional raft of showbiz luminaries. If these were the new, substantial heroes the commentators had promised, it seemed strange that they were being presented in a manner awfully like that of the old, vapid ones.

It was soon business as usual, quite literally. Thousands of New Yorkers may have died in a terrible event that ushered in a war of sorts between Western allies and Afghanistan's Taliban regime, but that was insufficient reason for the machinery of fame, with its attendant money-making properties, to grind to a halt. Indeed, voices within the entertainment industry even made the case that it was somehow patriotic to carry on consuming what the fame machine had to offer: it was an indirect means of asserting that fundamentalist terrorists would not change our way of life, no matter how stupefyingly trivial it might be.

So it was that within three months of the attacks on the World Trade Center and the Pentagon, people in the United States and other allied countries had flocked to see the first Harry Potter film and the first *Lord of the Rings* movie in such huge numbers that box office records tumbled. Their young lead actors (Daniel Radcliffe and Elijah Wood respectively) became new global stars. Tellingly these films, both conceived long before the horrors of 11 September, dealt in superhuman fantasy: they were an antidote and an escape from the mournful reality of real life.

Nothing was wrong in any of this. People have traditionally reached out for the solace of escapism in troubled times. But even if the attacks of 11 September had been ten or twenty times worse, they might not have been enough to stop the juggernaut of fame rolling ever on. Celebrity is a crucial adjunct of the entertainment industry, which has now grown to become one of the biggest and most lucrative in the world; for its wheels to stop turning would have huge, severe economic implications.

Then there is the fact the media and the entertainment industries have become closer in the last decade. Rupert Murdoch presides over one of the world's largest media companies as well as 20th Century-Fox, which encompasses a Hollywood film studio and a US television network. The publishing empire spearheaded by *Time* magazine is now formally in partnership with AOL and with Warner Bros. – another Hollywood studio, and also one of a handful of global record companies. Disney owns the ABC television network. Leaving aside considerations of editorial freedoms and independence within these companies, it is inescapably true that the entertainment industry, and more significantly its values, has muscled its way on to mainstream news agendas. News on US TV networks is subject to the same commercial imperatives as entertainment shows, and attracts the same sponsors and advertisers. It is thus crucial for news programmes to achieve high ratings by appealing to broad audiences. To networks that broadcast them, their function parallels that of entertainment shows: not to deliver news to a mass audience, but to deliver a mass audience to advertisers.

One of the best ways of achieving this is to make news programmes as entertaining as possible. Advertisers have long looked askance at drama series that might be deemed too depressing, complex or challenging. They want no excuse for viewers to reach for their remotes in search of something easier to digest. And they want to keep viewers, if not actively cheerful, then at least feeling sufficiently optimistic to consider purchasing their products: a contented viewer is a more susceptible consumer.

The usual manner of maximizing the entertainment value of news programming is the addition of glamour, gossip and celebrity. Upbeat clips of famous individuals on news broadcasts are thought to lift viewers' spirits and divert them from the pressing, harrowing issues of real life. How fortunate it is that news organizations can achieve this in a way that also benefits their new business partners: entities like Fox, Warner and Disney, with their endless production line of new movies, records and TV series, all of which benefit from prime-time plugs. Since modern fame is primarily an offshoot of the entertainment industry, and the entertainment industry has elevated itself to become an integral part of news agendas, there seems no reason in the foreseeable future why its progress should be halted. Certainly it will take more than one incident involving thousands of deaths and the destruction of two major New York skyscrapers.

Yet it is an odd paradox that while fame marches on, increasingly all-pervasive, the scope of ambition driving those who attain it have diminished drastically. In his book *The Frenzy of Renown*, which traces the beginnings of fame back to the days of Alexander the Great, Leo Braudy notes that the pursuit of fame was once tied to a greater ideal than mere self-aggrandizement; to Julius Caesar, for example, personal glory was indistinguishable from the glory his exploits brought to Rome.

It is certainly true that until the twentieth century fame was unanimously accepted as a by-product of extraordinary achievement. There was also an understanding that fame primarily involved being lauded and acknowledged in posterity, something more profound and satisfying than merely being well known during one's lifetime.

These ideas seem quaint and archaic in our modern culture, in which immediacy is all, and the prospect of delayed gratification – or no gratification at all during one's life – seems pointless. Increasingly, fame is merely about the individual who flaunts it. And an important factor in attaining modern fame seems to be an ambition for it; among aspirants to fame, the gulf between talent and desire has never seemed wider.

All this, allied to what the critic Robert Hughes calls the modern 'culture of complaint', makes contemporary fame unappetizing. In recent years there has been a remarkable increase in the number of famous people who have willingly and publicly disclosed their private problems – abusive parents, an unhappy childhood, problems with various addictions, a sense of victimhood about unfair discrimination. This could be construed as a canny instinct on their part that notoriety is today as interesting as 'positive' forms of fame, yet a thread common to many of their stories is that fame occurred as a result of driving ambition and raging desire. The attainment of celebrity is often regarded as a means not only to escape unhappiness early in life; it becomes a form of vindication, a compensation for past grievances, a redress for the unfairness of the hand originally dealt them. This is what modern fame can easily be reduced to. Not a desire to conquer new worlds, to make scientific breakthroughs, to improve the lot of the impoverished, or even to increase the sum of human happiness by entertaining others with art and skill, but all too often simply about making one person – the newly famous one – feel better inside. Call it fame as therapy.

So it is that the marginally gifted kids who apply to become members of manufactured pop groups on TV shows like *Pop Idol* routinely blame the callous, discourteous judges when they fail their audition. Inevitably, they are crushed by rejection. 'It's so unfair!' is their oft-heard mantra. They honestly appear to believe that their effort, ambition or desire are sufficient qualifications, rather than some spark of talent.

And so we sit, watching the swelling numbers of this passing parade of the briefly famous on our television screens. The most piteous may be those hapless, barely articulate guests on shows like Jerry Springer's, full of bile and simulated outrage as they tell tales of disappointment, betrayal and hurt with the intensity of actors up for an important audition. Rarely do they acquit themselves on TV as well as they seem to believe; yet this is their day in the sun, their one half-hour of fame before being dumped, unremembered, back into lifelong obscurity. Was it good for them? Do they feel healed? Has their appearance on television somehow validated them? One doubts it.

Nor does the appearance of contestants on shows like *Big Brother* or *Survivor* inspire confidence for their futures. Again, such programmes offer them a chance to indulge fantasies; they hope that prolonged exposure of their cheery, exhibitionist personalities will be found endearing by millions. But within weeks of the series finale, the participants are usually forgotten news. Actors on TV series and singers on pop videos seem to come and go at an ever more dizzying rate. We in the audience may rightly surmise that next year they will be reduced to guest spots on daytime game shows, and the year after their names will just be answers in nostalgia trivia quizzes.

Increasingly, we make these guesses consciously. The tendency of modern-day entertainment is to show us how the mechanisms of fame work. Many of us understand something these eager hopefuls choose to deny: that fame is merely a form of conveyor belt, with new faces moving along the line for our perusal, just as older ones are being ushered away from our gaze. We may be more dismissive about it now; we are certainly more knowing. In one sense, this may not be a terrible thing. It is probably healthier for society at large to understand fame's machinations rather than merely to be dazzled by it. We know something of the 'magic' of how movies are made, because we have seen so many behind-the-scenes TV programmes, often titled 'The Making Of . . .'. We understand the process of auditioning, of branding, market positioning and image-creation from fly-on-the-wall documentaries. Never in history have so many people been so savvy about the business of fame creation; more and more of us view it with one eyebrow ironically raised.

There is a serious point here. One wonders whether a population now sufficiently media-literate to recognize the shenanigans of spin doctors and the mechanics of propaganda will ever again be so vulnerable to the manipulations of would-be dictators with totalitarian ambitions. For example, would the German people so willingly have played along with Chancellor Hitler in the early 1930s if they had had the skill to deduce for themselves his real intentions and the hateful strategies that lay behind his rousing oratory? Maybe there is something to be said for the cheerful scepticism that attends modern-day fame, and the widespread understanding that it is finite and limited; such dismissiveness can act as a check on personality cults and those who would abuse power.

Even so, the democratization of fame carries a price. The primacy of individual opinion is unquestioned. From a wide variety of media, people who wish to inflict on the world their views, no matter how untouched by reality or common sense, trespass upon our lives. The guiding spirit behind radio call-in programmes is laudably democratic, yet they are hoist with their own petard; it is impossible for such shows to rise above the views of their most ignorant or bigoted callers. Of course, the most ignorant, bigoted voices to be heard are often those of the programme hosts; for some, like the Americans Rush Limbaugh and Howard Stern, the preferred way to achieve celebrity has been to express strong, loud opinions, usually of an extreme or distasteful nature, that pander to the audience's worst instincts.

The rise of interactive technology coincides with a new spirit of inclusiveness, giving audiences access to media forms (newspapers, radio, TV) previously denied them. Yet the opportunity is squandered: all too often people are asked to state their opinions on some trivial development in the fields of sports and entertainment, and the collating of views in the form of statistics ('24 per cent of our viewers think Sean Connery is the world's sexiest man'!) is depressingly meaningless. Such exercises can be actively distorting. One recalls with a shudder the daily polls conducted by some American TV covering the O. J. Simpson trial, which asked viewers for their opinions on how the trial was progressing, and whether, judging by Simpson's behaviour or body language in court, they perceived him as more guilty or less on any particular day. As if they were the jury, and this was some sort of popularity contest, rather than a murder case.

The video camera, another media form born out of democratic intent, has been effectively hijacked by those who would use it to press their claims to temporary fame. How many spontaneously funny domestic incidents recorded on video – babies falling over, fathers tripping over lawn mowers, wet dogs shaking themselves and soaking the family – have immediately been sent off to TV programmes consisting of precisely such clips? More to the point, how many of those supposedly spontaneous moments have been rehearsed, engineered or tailored to the demands of such TV shows? Such a question is irrelevant: the video camera, like the TV camera or the film camera, has the ability to make anyone who wanders into its frame look like a celebrity of sorts, no matter how modest his achievements.

And then there is the Internet, truly the most democratic form of all. Of course it is a wondrous development (the e-mail is one of the great boons of modern living) and many of its numerous applications are only beneficial. But at least in these early years of the World Wide Web, it is also raising an enormous problem relating to the value of the information it carries. For instance, people may read an item of news or information in a certain kind of publication – the *New York Times*, for example, or the *Economist* – and give it more credence than if they had read it in, say, a supermarket tabloid or a magazine containing pictures of naked women. The publication itself provides a context in which veracity may be assessed. The Internet currently provides no such context. Because of its democratic nature, anyone with a very modest amount of money can establish a website from which they can publish personal views, opinions and what may even look like news. How does the visitor to such a website discern the value of this information?

And of course the Internet is prey to people who would use it to assert their presence – indeed, their fame – in distorting ways. Matt Drudge started his gossipy website when he was an employee at the CBS gift shop in Burbank, California. When he overheard a juicy morsel of gossip, he posted it on his site, without feeling a need to verify facts or confirm sources. His renown gradually grew, but his big break came when he ran the gossip item that *Newsweek* magazine was sitting on a story about President Clinton's relationship with Monica Lewinsky. The appearance of this allegation on his website then became a story in itself; it was picked up by the conventional media, and ushered in a disturbing new era: gossip and rumour took their place right alongside verifiable facts in mainstream American reporting. Drudge set the tone for coverage of the entire Clinton scandal.

CONCLUSION

Unsurprisingly, the main beneficiary of all this was Drudge himself, who milked his new infamy for all it was worth. He turned out to be an inveterate fame-seeker, and even his sympathizers, such as journalist Michael Kinsley, claim he is less interested in issues than celebrity. Drudge also has an indifferent record, to put it mildly, on issues of accuracy. When he reported false rumours that President Clinton's aide Sidney Blumenthal beat his wife, Blumenthal responded with a $30 million lawsuit. Drudge has no editor, and therefore no one to mediate what he has to say, to rein him in, or order him to double check his facts and his sources. After the Lewinsky disclosures, everyone in America with a personal website, a set of strong opinions and a taste for fame suddenly wanted to be 'the new Matt Drudge'. But he has wielded a harmful influence. A decade ago, anyone in his line of work would have been derided as an unreliable charlatan; but his opportunistic use of the Internet has made him a star.

Another Internet star is Harry Knowles, a portly, ginger-haired young Texan who started the movie website ain't-it-cool-news. Knowles was not known for his silky social skills, and was initially regarded in Hollywood as something of a figure of fun. Yet he was tenacious. He arranged to smuggle a network of informants into preview screenings, and they then aired their views on his site about whether the movies matched the studios' hype. More often than not, they didn't, and at first the site incurred Hollywood's wrath. But soon Knowles was co-opted; studio executives who originally would not have given him a second glance invited him to receptions, courted him and made him feel as important as any established film critic. Eventually he became only too eager to dance to the studios' tune. Invited to spend two weeks in New Zealand on the set of *The Lord of the Rings*, he repaid the studio's hospitality by writing thirteen fawning, interminable pieces about how terrific the film would surely be: one for each day of his stay.

Any editor or mediating figure would have rejected the pieces as sub-standard drivel. Yet ain't-it-cool is visited daily by thousands of people presumably ignorant of the accommodations Knowles now makes with those he once mocked. Knowles has tried to shore up his image as a soft touch by attacking in advance a handful of weak, flawed films, but his site remains a fine example of opinion and information devoid of context or discipline. Still, it has made him a celebrity.

If people like Drudge, Knowles, Limbaugh and Stern can become famous, as well as the hapless contestants on reality TV, the talent-free adolescents on the 'create-a-pop-group' shows, and the warring dysfunctional families who blight the television landscape on programmes like Springer's, the question needs to be asked, is fame any longer worth having? Has it now become so pervasive and so debased that the sanest reaction for a sentient human being is to shrink from it?

There is no denying that fame can be a grubby business that chews up individuals, spits them out and moves impassively on. Its machinations make themselves evident in almost every area of human activity; fame creation is a growth industry, and its ceiling is, at the time of writing, nowhere in sight. The clamouring aspirations of those who would be famous, and the media's analysis of those aspirations, adds up to a Babel of voices, mostly spouting self-regarding trivia.

This may seem a harsh judgement, especially from one who makes a living partly from meeting and writing about famous people; the mere act of writing this book could be said to add to that Babel of voices. Yet I think there is a distinction to be drawn between an interest in fame itself and an interest in the minutiae of the lives of those who attain it – especially when it is attained despite a lack of talent or achievement.

Anyone who has interviewed even a few well-known actors will know that as a profession they tend to talk interminably about acting methods, and how they prepare for roles. The initial flush of delight at being in famous company recedes and the experience becomes commonplace; all that remains are dreary recitations of the technique involved in what is, after all, merely a craft. Famous actors often prefer to keep conversations with the media on this level, rather than discussing their star status or the possessions they have accrued. They seem faintly embarrassed by anything that impinges on their fame.

But I find increasingly that what I really want to know from famous people is how they feel about fame itself; not the number of houses they own, the lifestyle they enjoy, or the other famous people they befriend or date or sleep with, but how they hack their way through the thicket of celebrity. Is it more of a trial than a pleasure? Does it increase their sense of worth? Do they feel they deserve it? What strategies do they employ to cope with it? Do they fear its impending disappearance?

These all seem legitimate areas of serious enquiry. Fame is an obstacle to be negotiated, and sometimes a setback to be overcome. It can produce feelings of elation and satisfaction. Conversely, it can be a source of frustration, unhappiness and neurosis. The methods by which various people deal with it offer the potential of compelling narratives; any of them who have anything original or telling to say about it offer a small insight to the rest of us about how to live our lives. This, to some degree, is what we talk about when we talk about famous people.

As for the rest, well, it's merely a misplaced form of worship, much of it synthetically staged and whipped up by a compliant media with a vested interest in propagating the virtues of celebrityhood. But it must be apparent by now that fame brings with it profound drawbacks for each one of its advantages. Why have we allowed ourselves to become narcotized by its allure? How can value systems in so many areas of human endeavour have become so distorted by the tyranny of celebrity? Who are we deceiving but ourselves?

Index

abuse 35, 108, 116, 117, 135, 136
achievement 14, 15–16, 24–6, 49, 58, 62, 156
addiction 35, 36, 37
  alcohol 22, 30, 110, 129
  drugs 30, 38, 54, 64, 110–11, 117, 122, 129, 142
  sex 35
ain't-it-cool-news 161–2
Aitken, William Maxwell (Lord Beaverbrook) 16–17
Allen, Woody 48–9, 81, 89–90
ambition 156, 157
Ananova 82
Angeli, Pier 131
Angell, David 153
Anger, Kenneth 131
Arbuckle, Fatty 19, 22, 24
Armstrong, Neil 99
assassinations 44, 49–50, 53–4, 98
Assassins 53–4
Astaire, Fred 4
attention-seeking 28, 31–7, 118, 135
autograph hunters 42, 47, 105–6

Bardo, Robert John 50
Barnum, Phineas T. 19, 32
Barr, Roseanne 35
Bateman, Nick 73, 74
The Beatles 45, 95–8
Beatty, Warren 32, 66, 93–4
Beaverbrook, Lord 16–17
Beckham, Victoria 78, 127
Beecher-Moore, Nan 42–3, 71, 137
Belushi, John 54
Benatar, Pat 134
Berenson, Berry 153
Bertolucci, Bernardo 81
Best, George 110
Best, Pete 95
Big Brother 72–7, 158
Biograph Films 18, 20
Bjork 53
Blair, Euan 150
Blumenthal, Sidney 161
body language 47, 87, 89
Boorstin, Daniel 7, 32
Booth, John Wilkes 54
Bow, Clara 23
Bowie, David 33–4, 38–9, 89, 137, 139
Boyer, Charles 131
Branagh, Kenneth 59–61
Braudy, Leo 156
Britain 89, 90–91, 94–5, 97, 106, 129
Brown, Divine 130

Brown, Louise 99, 109
Bundy, Ted 54
Bush, George W. 87
Byron, Lord 14–15

Caine, Michael 63–4
Campbell, Joseph 61–2, 71, 72
Campbell, Naomi 142
Capshaw, Kate 120
Cara, Irene 8
Carlisle, Jo 78
Carter, Graydon 153, 154
Chaplin, Charlie 20, 21, 24
Chapman, Mark David 44, 49, 50, 53
charity work 75, 86, 119, 121, 138, 151
Charles, Prince 67, 99, 138, 149, 150–51
Charles, Ray 116
Cher 31, 50, 51
Chicago 18, 32
Chopra, Deepak 81
Clifford, Max 79
Clinton, Bill 31, 62, 66, 87, 117, 143–4, 145–6, 147, 148, 160
Cole, Nigel 2
Coleman, Allegra 81, 82
Collins, Joan 31
comebacks 61, 62–4, 65
confessions 35–7
Corrin, Tanya 83
Coward, Noël 77
Cox, Sara 142
Croft, Lara 82
Cruise, Tom 72, 80
Csikszentmihalyi, Mihaly 126, 127
Cunanan, Andrew 49
Curtis, Tony 45
Cusack, John 68–9, 88–9
cyberstars 82–3

Dafoe, Allan Roy 107–8
Daily Express 16–17, 25
Daily Mail 16, 151
Daily Telegraph 141
Dandridge, Dorothy 131
Day, Doris 79
Day of the Locust, The 47
de Becker, Gavin 50, 51–2
de Niro, Robert 154
Dean, James 15, 54, 55
death pools 54
deaths
　on 11 September 2001 153
　location tours 54
　premature 55, 152
　reactions to 54–6, 97
　see also assassinations; suicide
di Caprio, Leonardo 31
Diana, Princess of Wales 55, 66, 75, 97, 140, 141, 149, 150–52
Dietz, Dr Park 51
Dillon, Josephine 39–40
Dionne quintuplets 99, 107–9
Director, Roger 127, 128
Douglas, Michael 35, 142, 143
Downey Jr., Robert 35, 54, 64, 110–11
Dreyfuss, Richard 30–31
Drudge, Matt 160–61
Duvall, Robert 4, 118

Edward, Prince, Earl of Wessex 150
Eisenhower, Dwight D. 144–5
11 September 2001 153–5
Emin, Tracey 139
empathy 35, 36, 39, 62–3, 88, 97, 98
entertainment industry 10, 19, 155–6
　see also film industry
Entertainment Weekly 82

INDEX

entourages 6, 29–30, 38, 45, 136
Entwistle, Peg 55
Epstein, Brian 95–6
Esquire 61, 81
Evans, Andrew 130–31
Evans, Chris 65, 66
event relationships 66, 94

Fairbanks, Douglas 19, 20, 21–3
Falco, Edie 90–92
fame
   ambivalence towards 25, 89, 94, 129–30, 139, 151–2
   creation of 19, 24, 78–80, 158, 162
   dealing with 47, 89, 95–8, 162–3
   democratization of 158–9
   desire for 6–7, 13, 39, 73, 82–4, 94, 114, 126, 127, 134, 157
   disadvantages 6–8, 9, 12–13, 21–2, 26–7, 94, 126–7, 136–9
   as discrimination 105
   enthusiasm for 113–14, 116, 118, 122–5, 137
   increase of 7, 57
   overnight 38
   positive uses of 115–16, 117–18, 119, 120–21, 122
   pre-1900 14–16, 156
   process 58–60, 80, 106–7, 158
   as redemptive force 116, 120–21
   rejection of 25, 26, 38–9, 80, 103–6, 111–12
   as therapy 157
   transiency 8–9, 132–4, 157–9 (see also *Big Brother*)
   unique selling points 35
   see also involuntary fame
fans
   behaviour 44, 46, 91
   and celebrity deaths 54–6, 97
   community 45
   contempt for 44–5, 88
   encounters with 2–4, 21–2, 42–4, 45, 47, 88
   fan worship 45, 47
   hostility of 76
   illusion of intimacy 20–21, 43
   and image 46–7
   Internet sites 48
   mistrust of 44, 47, 49–50
   reasons for curiosity 57–8, 76
   relationship with 24, 42–3, 44–9
   uses of 47–8
   see also autograph hunters; stalkers
faux celebrities 78–84
Fayed, Dodi 152
fictional celebrities 81–2
Fielding, Helen 86
film critics 102, 128, 161
film industry
   celebrity 21–2
   heroes 72
   illusion of intimacy 20–21, 43
   influence of 92
   movie stars 18–20, 21, 27
   publicity stunts 18–19, 23
   regulation 22, 23
   sex appeal 22–3
Flockhart, Calista 140–41
Follmer, Brad 81–2
Fonda, Henry 64
Foster, Jodie 49
Fowles, Jib 37
Fox, Michael J. 51
Freud, Matthew 79
Fromm, Erich 33
Furnish, David 129

Gable, Clark 39–40
Gabler, Neal 32, 33

Gandhi, Mahatma 72, 93
Garbo, Greta 111
Geldof, Bob 120–21
ghoul pools 54
Gilmore, Gary 54
Giuliani, Rudy 154
Glyn, Elinor 23
Goldberg, Whoopi 1
gossip 76–7, 160
Graduate, The 104, 105, 106
Grant, Hugh 129–30
Griffith, D. W. 18, 20
Griffith, Melanie 37, 102
Ground Zero 153–4
guilt 35–6

Halliwell, Geri 65–6, 138
Hamilton, Ian 112
Hanks, Tom 91
happiness 126, 127, 139
Harmsworth, Alfred Charles (Lord Northcliffe) 16
Harris, Josh 83
Harris, Keith 132
Harrison, George 52, 96, 97, 98
Harry, Prince 150
Harry Potter 155
Hawking, Stephen 10–12, 109
Hawn, Goldie 1
Hear'Say 80–81
Hearst, Patty 100–103, 106–7
Hearst, William Randolph 17–18, 100, 102
Hello! 12, 69, 142, 143
Hemingway, Margaux 132
Hendrix, Jimi 55
Hepburn, Katharine 54, 134
hero myths 14, 58, 61–2, 71–2
Hill, Melanie 74–5
Hilton, Paris 154
Hinckley Jr., John W. 49, 50, 51, 53

Hoffman, Dustin 89, 104
Holly, Buddy 55
Holt, Nichola 74
Homer 134
homosexuality 25, 36, 66
Hooker, Matthew E. 52–3
Hooper, Nancy 52
Hopkins, Anthony 1
Houston, Whitney 115
Hudson, Rock 66
Hughes, Robert 157
Hutchence, Michael 121, 137

identity
  confusion 91, 92–3, 134–5
  re-invention 33–4, 93, 137–8
  sense of 6, 8, 10, 13, 35, 91, 95, 96, 132, 136–7
image 7, 8, 9–10, 32, 33–4, 46–7, 53, 62–3
Independent Motion Picture Company of America (IMP) 18–19, 20
Internet
  celebrity websites 37
  fan 'shrines' 48
  personal websites 52, 83–4, 160–62
  value of information 160
involuntary fame
  through association 147–8
  through heredity 99, 138–9, 150
  through kidnap 100–103, 106–7, 138
  through medical uniqueness 99, 107–9
  through photographs 99–100
  through work 99, 103–6, 107
  when fame turns sour 12–13, 109
  see also notoriety
Iungerich, Lauren 81–2

INDEX

Jackson, Andrew 1
Jackson, Michael 70, 93, 134–6
Jagger, Mick 15, 122–5
James, Clive 136–7
Jennicam 83–4
John, Elton 64, 128–9
Johnson, Ian 81
Johnson, Lyndon 144
Johnson, Richard 154
Jones, Paula 144, 147
Jones, Tom 46–7
Judd, Ashley 52

Kay, Richard 151
Kennedy, Jacqueline 99
Kennedy, John Fitzgerald 53, 72, 99, 143–4, 145
Kennedy Jr., John 99
Keppel, Judith 67, 68
Keystone 20, 22
Kidman, Nicole 52–3, 140
kidnappings 26, 51, 101–3, 138
Kilmer, Val 128
Kingsley, Ben 92–3
Kingsley, Pat 79
Kinsley, Michael 161
Knowles, Harry 161–2
Kopple, Barbara 48

Ladd, Alan 131
Laemmle, Carl 18–19
Larter, Ali 81
Lawrence, Florence 18–19
Lawrence, T. E. 24–5, 89
Leaming, Barbara 133
Lennon, John 38, 44, 49, 95, 96
Leno, Jay 130
Letterman, David 52, 68–9, 84
Lewinsky, Monica 66, 144, 147–9, 160
Lewis, Jerry 52

Limbaugh, Rush 159
Lindbergh, Anne Morrow 26
Lindbergh, Charles 25–7
Livingstone, David 15–16
London 89, 90–91, 94–5, 97
lookalikes 132
Lopez, Jennifer 32
Lopez, Ricardo 53
Lord of the Rings 155, 161
Los Angeles 79, 94
Lucas, George 62, 71

Ma Maison 133
Madonna 5, 32–3, 34, 51, 52, 66, 93–5, 110, 137, 140
magazines 77, 78–9, 141–2, 149, 153, 154
Mailer, Norman 54
Maloney, Michael 134
Maltin, Leonard 102
Manson, Charles 49
marriage 12, 21, 59–60, 64–5, 122
Martin, Steve 42, 49
McCall, Davina 74
McCarthy, Cormac 112
McCartney, Paul 95, 96, 97, 98
McCaughey septuplets 108
McInerney, Jay 61
media 9, 10, 155–6
    see also magazines; newspapers; photographs; radio call-in programmes; story-telling; television
mediathons 66
Mellor, David 146–7
Mills, Gordon 46
Mirror 142
Mitterand, François 143
The Monkees 80
Monroe, Marilyn 31, 131, 134
Moonlighting 128

Moore, Demi 29–30
morality 69–70, 93, 119–21, 135–6, 145
Morrison, Jim 15, 55
Morton, Andrew 148, 151
Moyers, Bill 71
Muhammad Ali 93
Murdoch, Rupert 155
Musician 124

Nash, Ogden 23
Neeson, Liam 92
New York 91, 94, 95, 97
New York Journal 17–18
New York Post 154
New York Times 66, 148, 154
New York World 17
Newman, Paul 80, 137
newspapers
    attracting readership 16–18, 22, 25, 26–7, 77–8, 94, 141–2, 146, 149
    and 11 September 2001 154
    film critics 128
    interviews 9–10, 87
    reputation 160
    story-telling 58–9, 60, 61, 67–8
    see also paparazzi
Nicholson, Viv 68
Niven, David 39
Nixon, Richard 62, 122
Nolan, Anna 74
Northcliffe, Lord 16
notoriety 21, 22, 23, 109–11, 130, 135, 157

OK! 12, 143
O'Shea, Caroline 74
Oswald, Lee Harvey 53, 54

Paltrow, Gwyneth 52

paparazzi 55, 95, 110, 111, 140–42, 149, 152
paranoia 5, 50, 51, 100
Parker Bowles, Camilla 67, 151
Parton, Dolly 51, 113–16, 125
Penn, Sean 110
personality
    disorders 28–9, 35, 37, 40–41, 53, 135–6
    and fame 37–8, 40
    presidential traits 40
Pfeiffer, Michelle 43
philanthropy 117, 119–20
Phillips, Craig 74, 75
photographs 99–100, 112, 141–3, 149–50
    see also paparazzi
Pickford, Mary 19, 20, 21–2
Piper, Billie 52
Pitt, Brad 52
politicians 51–2, 71–2, 145–7
    see also presidents
Popstars 80–81
Power, Tyrone 45
presidents
    assassinations 53–4
    personality traits 40
    public interest 143–6, 147
    role-playing 87
    sexual liaisons 144–5, 147
Presley, Elvis 45, 55, 56, 97, 115, 123, 135, 136
Presley, Lisa Marie 135
privacy
    ambivalence towards 25, 83, 89–90, 151–2
    court actions 108, 142–3, 161
    European Human Rights Act 142–3
    France 143
    invasions of 7, 68–9, 91, 94, 147–50

INDEX

politicians 143–7
  in public 47, 89–90, 97
  and public interest 143–7
  reclusivity 111–12
  respect for 97, 150
  royalty 140, 149–52
  United States 50, 147–9
  see also fans; paparazzi
propaganda 158–9
publicists 79–80
publicity 18–19, 23, 68, 96, 151
Pulitzer, Joseph 17

Radcliffe, Daniel 155
radio call-in programmes 159
Ramsay, Darren 74, 75
Rapp, Virginia 22
Reagan, Ronald 49, 87, 96, 122
Redford, Robert 51
Reeves, George 131
Reeves, Jim 55–6
relationships 59–61, 66, 69, 83, 94
religion 57, 71, 119–20
Remington, Frederic 18
Rich, Frank 66, 148
Ringley, Jennifer 83–4
Rivers, Joan 50–51
Roberts, Julia 1–4, 72, 80
Roberts, Yvonne 137
Rock, Chris 154
rock tours 123–4
role-playing 3, 11, 25, 43, 69, 85–9, 90, 93–4, 95, 98, 103, 132
The Rolling Stones 45, 54, 122–4
Ronstadt, Linda 52
Roosevelt, Franklin D. 145
Roosevelt, Theodore 121
Rose, Axl 52
Rosen, Jeffrey 147, 148
royalty 99, 140, 149–52

Rudd, Eve (Fred) 104–6
Ryan, Jeri 52

Salinger, J. D. 112
Sanders, George 131
Sarandon, Susan 154
Schindler's List 92, 93, 118, 120
Schulberg, B. P. 23
Schwimmer, David 81
Seberg, Jean 131
security 47, 50–52, 96–7
self-absorption 28, 29–31, 33, 127–31, 137
Sennett, Mack 20, 22
sex-appeal 22–3, 46, 134
Shaeffer, Rebecca 50
Shakespeare, William 71, 134
Shaw, George Bernard 25
Shepherd, Cybill 128
Shields, Brooke 52
Siegel, Peggy 79
Simpson, O. J. 66, 69–70, 159
Sinatra, Frank 45, 62, 64
Sinatra Jr., Frank 138–9
Skank 81–2
Sondheim, Stephen 53
Sopranos, The 90–91
Spears, Britney 32
Spice Girls 32, 65, 78, 138
Spielberg, Arnold 118, 120
Spielberg, Steven 4, 11, 92, 118–20
sponsorship 26
Stalin, Josef 4–5
stalkers 50, 51, 52–3, 142
Stanley, Henry Morton 15–16
Stansfield, Lisa 127
Star Wars 62, 71
Starr, Kenneth 147, 148
Starr, Ringo 96
Stern, Howard 52, 159
Stone, Sharon 52

story-telling 14, 16–17, 57, 58–9, 61–72, 148–9, 150–51
Streisand, Barbra 52, 80, 133
suicide 37, 54–5, 131–2, 137
Sullavan, Margaret 131
Sun 81
Sunday People 142
Survivor 72, 158
Survivors of the Shoah Visual History Foundation 120

T-babe 82
Tarantino, Quentin 63
Tate, Sharon 49
Taylor, Derek 98
Taylor, Elizabeth 31, 64–5
television
    attracting audiences 77–8, 149, 155–6
    court cases 69, 159
    documentaries 1–2
    interviews 87–8
    news programmes 155–6
    pop groups 80–81, 157, 158
    quiz shows 67
    reality shows 65, 72–7
    story-telling 58–9
    syntax of 85–6
    talk shows 35, 68–9, 80, 84, 87–9, 117, 121, 130, 157–8
    video clips 160
Temple, Shirley 121–2
Thomas, Lowell 24–5
Thompson, Emma 59–61
Thornton, Billy Bob 117–18, 125
Tigress Productions 1
Time magazine 100, 155
Tinseltown Studios 86
Todd, Thelma 39
Tomb Raider 82
Travolta, John 63

Truth or Dare 32
Turner, Tina 51
Tyson, Mike 109–10

United Artists 20

Valentino, Rudolph 25, 55
Vanity Fair 117, 153, 154
Velez, Lupe 131
Versace, Gianni 49
video cameras 159–60
violence 36, 109–10

Waters, John 101–2
weaknesses 31, 35–7, 75, 134
Webb, Charles 103–6, 107
websites *see* Internet
Weidman, John 53
WeLiveInPublic.com 83
Welles, Orson 100, 118, 132–4
West, Nathanael 47
Who Wants To Be A Millionaire? 67–8
William, Prince 150
Williams, Esther 45, 47
Williams, Hank 55
Williams, Robbie 65, 66
Williams, Robin 1, 54
Willis, Bruce 61, 80, 128
Wilson, Earl 46
Wilson, Glenn D. 130–31
Winfrey, Oprah 116–17, 125
Winslet, Kate 141
Wonder, Stevie 116
Wood, Elijah 155
Wright, Robin 110

Yates, Paula 121, 137
Young, Gig 131

Zeta-Jones, Catherine 142, 143
Zukor, Adolph 20